5217/01011186/17/6/02

AF758511

UNIVERSITY OF NORTHUMBRIA
AT NEWCASTLE LIBRARY
WITHDRAWN

PAEDIATRICS

Cavendish
Publishing
Limited

London • Sydney

TITLES IN THE SERIES

ACCIDENT AND EMERGENCY

CARDIOLOGY

CLINICAL CARE

DENTISTRY

EAR, NOSE AND THROAT

ELDERLY CARE MEDICINE

GENERAL PRACTICE

GYNAECOLOGY

MEDIATION AND ARBITRATION

NEPHROLOGY

NEUROLOGY

OBSTETRICS

ONCOLOGY

OPHTHALMOLOGY

PAEDIATRICS

PSYCHIATRY

RESPIRATORY DISORDERS

UROLOGY

VASCULAR SURGERY

PAEDIATRICS

SJ Rose MA, MB BChir, FRCPCH, FRCP, MD
Consultant Paediatrician,
Birmingham Heartlands Hospital

SERIES EDITOR
Dr Walter Scott, LLB (Hons), MBBS, MRCGP, DObstRCOG

Cavendish
Publishing
Limited

London • Sydney

First published in Great Britain 2002 by Cavendish Publishing Limited, The Glass House, Wharton Street, London WC1X 9PX, United Kingdom

Telephone: +44 (0) 20 7278 8000 Facsimile: +44 (0) 20 7278 8080

Email: info@cavendishpublishing.com

Website: www.cavendishpublishing.com

© Rose, SJ 2002

UNIVERSITY OF NORTHUMBRIA AT NEWCASTLE LIBRARY

ITEM No.	CLASS No.
2004478446	618.92 ROS

All rights reserved. No part of this publication may be reproduced, stored in a retrieval system, or transmitted, in any form or by any means, electronic, mechanical, photocopying, recording, scanning or otherwise, except under the terms of the Copyright Designs and Patents Act 1988 or under the terms of a licence issued by the Copyright Licensing Agency, 90 Tottenham Court Road, London W1P 9HE, UK, without the permission in writing of the publisher.

British Library Cataloguing in Publication Data

Rose, SJ

Paediatrics – (Medico-legal practitioner series)

1 Paediatrics 2 Paediatrics – law and legislation

I Title

618.9'2

ISBN 1 85941 698 5

Printed and bound in Great Britain

FOREWORD

When I first conceived the idea of the *Medico-Legal Practitioner Series* in the summer of 1994, I had been preparing reports for lawyers on cases of alleged medical negligence for about five years. I had also been looking at other doctors' reports for the same length of time and it was becoming increasingly apparent to me that one of the lawyers' most difficult tasks was to understand the medical principles clearly. To be fair to the lawyers, there were some doctors who did not always make matters very clear. This, coupled with the difficulty which many doctors have in understanding the legal concept of negligence and related topics, merely served to compound the problem.

Nearly five years have now passed since I wrote the foreword for the initial launch of the series and we now have nearly a score of titles available. Therefore, this seems to be an appropriate moment to take stock of our efforts so far and to assess the way in which matters are likely to unfold in the future.

Since the publication of the first books in the series, there have been some exciting developments in the medico-legal scene and there can be no doubt that this is becoming an increasingly specialised field. That trend has become firmly entrenched with the establishment of legal aid franchise firms of lawyers. Such firms will find it more and more necessary to identify strong cases and eliminate weak ones in an economical fashion and with as little risk as possible.

One important feature of the more recent titles in the series is the inclusion of case studies which are placed adjacent to the relevant parts of the text and are listed in a table for ease of reference. Most chapters have several examples of cases which have either settled in the claimant's favour or have fallen away because, perhaps, they were considered to be weak on negligence or causation. These studies give the reader a 'feel' for the work of the clinician and the difficulties which face him. The patient's expectations do not always correlate particularly well with the doctor's treatment plan, for example, in relation to consent, and such issues as this are often highlighted by the case studies.

The other interesting development in some of the newer titles is the coverage of areas that do not relate to clinical negligence. With the series becoming more comprehensive, we have felt able to expand into other medico-legal areas. Examples include *Respiratory Disorders*, which deals with industrial lung disease, and *Psychiatry*, which covers testamentary capacity and the defence of insanity to criminal charges.

So much, then, for the latest developments in the *Medico-Legal Practitioner Series*. Our aim remains as it was at the outset with regard to uniformity of approach and clarity of presentation. In this way, I hope that our readers, mostly the practitioners who are engaged in unravelling the complexities of the medical evidence that is the subject of so much litigation, will continue to rely on us as an invaluable source of reference.

Walter Scott
Series Editor
Slough
January 2002

PREFACE

The first 18 years of life witness greater change than in any age group. Infants and children can be assaulted by a bewildering variety of illnesses which can vary according to their age and size.

This book attempts to explain the basics of paediatric practice and the rationale for medical decisions from the neonatal period to adulthood. The first part of the book relates to the neonatal period, initially following a chronological pathway from before birth to the first few days of life, and then moving on to abnormalities that may either be present at birth or which become more obvious in the first few weeks and months of life.

Children's medical requirements are for most of their life met by general practitioners. A small percentage of children need more specialised care in district general hospitals and an even smaller percentage need the highly specialised care afforded by tertiary paediatric units. The nature of the interaction between these three areas of care and the pitfalls that can occur when transferring between these levels of care are explored. Thereafter I follow an 'organ' approach to the general underlying principles of paediatric care.

I have tried to illuminate the many difficulties faced by clinicians by using examples taken from my own practice, both clinical and medico-legal. In this way I hope I have been able to make clearer the decision making processes that are undertaken in neonatal and paediatric practice and how errors in either clinical judgment or clinical practice can occur.

Dr SJ Rose
January 2002

CONTENTS

CHAPTER 1

RESUSCITATION

INTRODUCTION

The first breath an infant takes is, unsurprisingly, of enormous importance. This breath converts the lungs from a collapsed, fluid-filled state to an expanded air-filled system capable of gas exchange. The infant creates a large negative pressure during this first breath in order to drag air into the lungs. The baby needs to be in good condition after the several hours of the birth process in order to establish an independent life. If the infant is not in sufficiently good condition to survive without intervention, we need to be able to assess the infant in order to institute appropriate resuscitation measures.

TYPES OF FACILITIES REQUIRED

There are three categories of neonatal care, termed intensive care, high dependency and special care. Intensive care and high dependency are centralised facilities, so maternity units have differing on-site neonatal care. Those maternity units with only special care baby facilities should only deliver low-risk pregnancies; high-risk pregnancies should be transferred to a maternity unit with on-site intensive care facilities. However, low-risk pregnancies can go wrong and also women may present in pre-term but advanced labour, which precludes transfer. It is better to deliver a premature baby in any maternity unit than in an ambulance.

All maternity units must, therefore, have a safety net so that high-risk babies can be resuscitated and stabilised until they can be transferred to an intensive care unit. The vast majority of maternity units have a neonatal medical team to provide this safety net. A junior paediatric doctor should be present at high-risk births, or be available virtually immediately if low-risk pregnancies produce high-risk babies. There are some midwife-led maternity units or units without on-site paediatric cover. These units must have a policy for coping with the unexpected. There is not a unified approach; some units rely on a fast response from the local neonatal unit and others have midwives trained in resuscitation skills. Whatever the system, it must allow deliveries in a safe environment and be able to cope, at least short term, with unexpected complications.

There must be facilities to resuscitate and stabilise the baby before transfer to the intensive care unit. However, the vagaries of medicine mean that it can be several hours, and occasionally days, before the baby can be transferred. If things go wrong during this period, the care delivered by the special care baby unit must be judged by the standards of similar units, not by the standards of the centralised intensive care units that have considerably more expertise, equipment and personnel.

ASSESSMENT BY APGAR SCORE

The assessment of a new-born baby is by the Apgar score. The Apgar score is a numerical description of the baby, given at one, five and 10 minutes of life. Five features are scored from 0 to 2 (see Table 1). The one-minute Apgar score is used to determine the necessary resuscitation measures. However, clinically the main features assessed are heart rate, respiratory effort and colour. If the heart rate is less than 100 beats per minute (bpm) with poor or absent respiratory effort, then active resuscitation will be required. A baby who is not breathing is called apnoeic: this may be either blue or white apnoea.

Table 1: Apgar score

Sign	**0**	**1**	**2**
Heart rate	Absent	<100 bpm	>100 bpm
Respiratory effort	Absent	Weak	Good
Muscle tone	Limp	Some flexion of limbs	Active movement
Reflex irritability	None	Grimace to stimulation	Cry to stimulation
Colour	White	Blue	Pink

RESUSCITATION MEASURES

Resuscitation takes place on a resuscitaire that has facilities for keeping the baby warm, administering oxygen and allowing suction of the baby. There is also a clock for the timing of Apgar scores, equipment to effect intubation, and certain drugs necessary for resuscitation. The resuscitaire must be checked regularly by nursing staff, but it is the absolute responsibility of the attending paediatrician to make sure that all the equipment is present and working before the birth of the baby. It is indefensible for a paediatrician to blame nursing staff if equipment is not working, except in the circumstance of a crash call when the paediatrician arrives to resuscitate a baby after it is born.

Ventilation

If the Apgar score is low, equal to or less than 3, then active intervention is necessary. In blue apnoea, resuscitation may be possible with bag and mask or T-piece ventilation, when oxygen is forced into the lungs. In white, or terminal, apnoea the baby is in a far worse state and will only respond to intubation, placing a tube directly into the lungs. Ventilation of the lungs, and therefore improving oxygenation, is affected by intermittent positive pressure being applied either via the face mask or tube. Care must be taken, though, to avoid applying too great a pressure. There are two oxygen outlets on a resuscitaire, only one of which can be pressure-regulated. The unregulated outlet is used to give added oxygen to a self-ventilating baby; only the pressure-regulated outlet should be used for intermittent positive pressure ventilation. An adjustable pressure gauge regulates this outlet. Failure to use this regulator, or over zealous use of the bag, could result in the baby's lungs being subjected to very high gas pressures with consequent damage: pneumothoraces.

Drug therapy and cardiac massage

Adequate oxygenation of the infant also requires a satisfactory circulation, and therefore an acceptable heart rate, which is defined as greater than 100 bpm. External cardiac massage may be necessary to maintain adequate circulation, which will automatically improve when oxygenated blood circulates through the body. However, on occasions the heart rate will not improve and other resuscitation procedures are necessary. Adrenaline can be administered down the endotracheal tube, allowing rapid absorption. It is probably not necessary to give adrenaline directly into the heart, as this is a more difficult and hazardous method of administration when the endotracheal tube is readily available.

Whilst waiting for the adrenaline to have an effect, continued cardiac massage might be necessary. A new-born baby's rib cage is very soft so care must be taken to avoid over-vigorous cardiac massage, which can physically bruise the heart and, on occasion, rupture the heart muscle.

There is little published evidence that correcting the build-up of acid in the baby during poor oxygenation is of benefit. However, if adrenaline and cardiac massage have not been successful then sodium bicarbonate can be used. This must be given intravenously, and in a collapsed baby the umbilical vein is the easiest route. An equal volume of fluid should ideally dilute the sodium bicarbonate; if this is not available, undiluted sodium bicarbonate must be infused slowly.

Acute blood loss

One obstetric emergency is ante-partum haemorrhage, which means that the placenta has come away from the wall of the womb. This causes an interruption of the oxygen supply from the mother to the fetus. This can lead to a severely compromised baby at birth. The blood lost during an ante-partum haemorrhage mainly comes from the mother; however, the fetus can also lose blood, which again compromises the oxygenation of the fetal tissues. Recognition of the difference between a pale baby caused by white apnoea as opposed to haemorrhage is difficult, but the presence of an ante-partum haemorrhage should alert the attending doctor to the possibility of fetal anaemia. This requires urgent unmatched blood transfusion, normally via an umbilical vein catheter.

CESSATION OF RESUSCITATION

The most difficult decision is to stop resuscitation. The Apgar score indicates the immediate condition of the baby and the resuscitation requirements. If there is no improvement, or indeed no heartbeat at all, then a decision is necessary as to whether it is appropriate to continue resuscitation, with the possibility of a baby surviving with severe neurological damage, or whether cessation of resuscitation is the correct action. This decision should be made by the most senior paediatrician present, and may require telephone discussions with the consultant. There are no accepted guidelines as to the time limit for continuing resuscitation as, frequently, the state of the fetus during the minutes before birth is unknown. Thus a baby who presents in a parlous state may have been in trouble for some time, or may have just been compromised, for example, if the umbilical cord is suddenly compressed. As these two scenarios cannot always be separated, there can be no proscriptive comments about cessation of resuscitation. However, it is generally accepted that if no sustained heartbeat can be achieved by 15 minutes of life, continued resuscitation is not appropriate.

OUTCOME PREDICTION

The one-minute Apgar score has no relevance for eventual outcome and cannot be used to predict the neurological outcome for any particular baby.

Indeed, the Apgar scores at any time taken alone are of little use for outcome prediction. The most useful is the five-minute score, but even this should be combined with other features to improve prediction.

Many such additional features have been considered. One is the passage of meconium (fetal stool) in the womb. This is relatively unhelpful, as meconium can be passed normally by term or post-term infants born in the breech position, bottom first. The passage of meconium by the pre-term infant, whose gut should not be working, does have greater correlation with fetal distress, but has poor correlation with outcome.

The difficulty in utilising individual assessments to predict long term outcome has led to various authors attempting to develop scoring systems that attempt to link immediate postnatal events in the baby with long term outcome. It is also important to develop a system that tries to differentiate between ante- and perinatal events. Several of these systems are discussed in Chapter 3, Perinatal Asphyxia.

Case study: unrecognised faulty equipment causing the unnecessary death of a new-born baby

The on-call paediatric senior house officer received an urgent call to the labour ward to resuscitate a flat baby. The senior house officer decided to resuscitate the baby by bag-and-mask ventilation. He chose the appropriate sized mask and attached the bag to both oxygen and the mask. Despite ventilation, the baby did not improve. He decided to intubate the baby and called for senior assistance. Despite the efforts of both paediatricians, the baby's heart rate could not be maintained. At post mortem it was discovered that the baby had bilateral large pneumothoraces which had not been diagnosed ante mortem. The resuscitation equipment was checked and it was discovered that the blow-off valve was stuck. This valve limits the amount of pressure which can be generated in the bag.

The claimants argued that the faulty valve caused the pneumothoraces, that the fault should have been recognised by the paediatricians, and further that they were negligent in not diagnosing the pneumothoraces. Had there been recognition of the pneumothoraces, then treatment could have easily been instituted and the baby would have survived. The hospital did not contend the case.

CHAPTER 2

BIRTH TRAUMA

INTRODUCTION

The passage of the fetus through the birth canal, having to traverse the inflexible bony pelvis, can be traumatic to both mother and fetus. The mode of presentation, whether head first, face first or feet first, has implications for the likelihood of fetal damage, which can be to the head, nerves, soft tissues or bones. The use of rigid instrumentation, such as forceps or Ventouse extraction, adds to the possibility of trauma.

CENTRAL NERVOUS SYSTEM TRAUMA

The central nervous system consists of the brain and spinal cord. Traumatic damage is generally mechanical, causing damage either by direct effect, or indirectly via inducing haemorrhage, which then causes the damage.

The birth process itself demands squeezing and moulding of the head in order to traverse the bony pelvis. There are also movements at the neck to facilitate passage through the birth canal. Different presentations, that is, face first, brow first, feet first, etc, also create difficulties as discussed in obstetric textbooks. Thus natural, unassisted childbirth can be associated with trauma to the fetus. However, the use of rigid instrumentation to assist birth increases the risk of trauma, so appropriate techniques must be used to minimise that risk.

Mechanical trauma

The use of different types of forceps and their indications have varied with evolving obstetric practice. However, recent reports suggest that between 15% and 20% of deliveries are assisted by forceps or Ventouse extraction.

Ventouse extraction is effected by applying a suction cap to the head, then creating a vacuum to a pre-set limit, so firmly attaching the suction cap to the scalp. The vacuum produced can cause local damage, with swelling of the underlying skin, a chignon, which normally resolves rapidly. However, unless care is taken, the suction cap can come away from the skin of the scalp if strong traction is applied, producing shearing forces in the underlying skin. Such trauma to the scalp can lead to a large area of skin loss, which may require skin grafting with permanent hair loss in that area.

Skull structure

The plates of the skull meet along suture lines. Where the suture line traverses the top of the skull there are two soft areas, fontanelles: an anterior fontanelle and a posterior fontanelle. If the part of the skull presenting first during birth includes the fontanelle, and this is not recognised during vaginal examination, the Ventouse unit may be inappropriately applied directly over the fontanelle. There have been reports of the fontanelle tissue being sucked up into the suction cap and with it brain tissue, causing considerable local brain damage.

There is no doubt that a highly traumatic forceps delivery can damage both mother and child. The forceps may be misapplied, covering the face and back of the head, allowing crushing forces to be applied to the head rather than forming a protective cage around it. Misapplied or inappropriately applied forceps can cause direct damage both to the skull, causing fractures, and to the underlying brain tissue. However, even though there may have been sufficient force to cause fractures, direct trauma to brain tissue is relatively uncommon and should raise the possibility of lack of due care in the use of forceps.

Spinal cord trauma

Considerable longitudinal force can be applied when using forceps and, to a lesser extent, when using Ventouse extraction, as overcoming the suction acts as a form of safety valve. The spinal cord in a baby is fixed at both ends, one obviously a continuation of the brain, the other end tethered to the base of the spinal canal. A baby's spine is relatively elastic and can be stretched by 4–4.5 cm without harm and without dislocation of individual bones. However, the spinal cord itself is not so pliable and is unable to stretch to the same degree, probably no more than 0.8–1.0 cm, so will snap if too much traction is applied.

Signs of spinal cord transection

Excessive force during assisted delivery has the potential, therefore, of transecting the fetus's spinal cord. This usually happens at a high level, somewhere in the neck. If the level is very high the diaphragm is paralysed and the baby cannot breathe. Spinal cord transection is rare, so the attending paediatrician is highly unlikely to diagnose this problem, considering that a non-breathing baby merely needs adequate resuscitation before breathing will commence. Sadly, once the diagnosis is made there is nothing available other than withdrawal of intensive care. If the transection occurs lower down in the neck, the baby will be able to breathe but will be completely paralysed from the neck downwards.

Spinal column trauma

Extreme traction transmitted to the spine via forceps will eventually lead to dislocation of the spinal joints, effectively breaking the baby's neck, for which there can be no justification.

Intra-cranial haemorrhage

Intra-cranial haemorrhages are uncommon but are reported following the use of both forceps and Ventouse extraction. The commonest variety, subdural haemorrhage, occurs just outside the surface of the brain and is caused by rupture of the connecting veins or venous sinuses. Venous sinuses are large blood vessels in the skull but outside the brain matter. There are connecting veins from the veins on the surface of the brain to these sinuses. It is the connecting veins that can be ruptured by trauma. The incidence of subdural haemorrhage is thought to be around two per 1,000 births. The damage to the brain is caused by a pressure effect from the bleeding, which then compromises blood flow and oxygen delivery to brain tissue.

Again, traumatic forceps deliveries will cause bleeding as well as direct damage. There are, however, case reports of subdural haemorrhages occurring after apparently uncomplicated instrumental deliveries, indicating that it is difficult to determine whether bleeding was caused by instrumentation or by the fetal problem which led to the use of forceps.

There is some evidence that being born in the breech position increases the incidence of subdural haemorrhage. The chest is compressed whilst travelling through the pelvis, and this causes a raised pressure in the veins in the head. As the head is compressed in the pelvis the pressure in the veins increases further, which can result in rupture of the veins or sinuses. Some obstetricians apply forceps to the after-coming head, especially in premature infants. In such instances it becomes virtually impossible to determine whether any subdural bleed was caused by being born breech or by dangerous use of forceps.

PERIPHERAL NERVE TRAUMA

There are two common types of peripheral nerve injury: facial nerve injury and brachial plexus injury. The facial nerve comes out of the skull in front of the ear and spreads over the jawbone into the face. It can therefore be damaged by pressure of the forceps crushing it against the underlying bone.

The brachial plexus is made up of several nerve roots that come together and subsequently split into the nerves to the arm and hand. Damage is caused by stretching or transection of the nerves.

Facial nerve injury

Facial nerve injury appears to relate almost entirely to the use of forceps for delivery. This can either be mid-cavity or low forceps. The incidence therefore varies directly with the incidence of forceps delivery. The use of forceps has diminished considerably over the last 15 years, and also the types of forceps utilised have altered. Some units now use Ventouse delivery in preference to forceps. However, a paper reviewing the incidence of facial nerve injury following forceps delivery suggested a rate of 7.5 per 1,000: 1 in 133. Fortunately, the majority are caused by direct bruising and complete and spontaneous recovery normally obtains.

Brachial plexus injury

The incidence of brachial plexus injury causing Erb's palsy is quoted as around 2.6 per 1,000, or 1 in 385 single full-term pregnancies.

The nerves emanating from the spinal cord in the neck, collectively known as C5-C8 and T1, form the brachial plexus. This plexus innervates the muscles in the arm and hand. The nerves descend between the muscles in the neck, under the collarbone and into the arm through the armpit. There are many branches from the plexus to different muscles in the arm, but the two main nerves are the median nerve, C5-C6, and the ulnar nerve, C8-T1.

The median nerve supplies the muscles that enable us to lift the arm, bend the elbow and move the wrist. The ulnar nerve supplies the muscles to the hand. Damage to these nerves during birth causes paralysis or palsy that can be temporary or permanent.

Erb's palsy

Damage to the median nerve causes Erb's palsy. This results in the arm hanging limply by the side of the body, the palm of the hand facing backwards and the fingers curved, the so called 'waiter's tip' sign. The fingers move normally unless there is some damage to the lower nerve roots, when finger movement is affected.

Klumpke's palsy

Damage to the ulnar nerve causes Klumpke's palsy, when forearm and finger movements are compromised. Erb's palsy is far more common than Klumpke's palsy. This is related to the mode of damage to the nerves caused by lateral flexion of the neck during vertex delivery. Both palsies can occur following breech delivery, when the arm is extended above the head, causing traction on the nerves in the armpit.

SHOULDER DYSTOCIA

Normal spontaneous vertex delivery means that the baby's head is born first. The head is flexed against the chest so the back of the head is the first part born, opening up the birth canal. The head is the part of the fetal body with the largest diameter so, in theory, if the head can pass through the bony pelvis then the rest of the body slips through when the midwife exerts gentle downward traction on the head. This actually means that the neck is flexed sideways, as the baby's face is towards the inner aspect of the mother's thigh. This creates tension on the nerves and muscles of the upper side of the neck. However, there are occasions when the shoulders get stuck (shoulder dystocia) and the birth process stops.

The pelvis is joined together at the front by the pubic bone. The baby's anterior shoulder gets stuck behind the pubic bone and, as the womb undergoes the next contraction to expel the rest of the baby and the midwife pulls down on the head, the shoulder becomes further impacted behind the pubic bone. This is a highly dangerous situation, as the umbilical cord may be compressed between the bony pelvis and the fetus's chest, causing oxygen starvation to the baby. Somehow the baby must be delivered rapidly in order to prevent brain damage or death.

Shoulder dystocia is more common in large babies, greater than 4 kg, but can occur in small babies also. Estimating a baby's weight in the womb is hopelessly inaccurate, so shoulder dystocia cannot be predicted and therefore occurs suddenly and unexpectedly. Thus clear guidelines for methods of coping with shoulder dystocia are mandatory in all obstetric units.

Diagnosis of shoulder dystocia

Shoulder dystocia is a highly unpredictable complication of birth. Clues to its diagnosis are: the head moving back up the birth canal after a contraction when delivery could be anticipated; a failure of restitution, that is, the head turning towards the mother's thigh after delivery; and finally the failure to deliver the baby's body once the head has been delivered.

Treatment of shoulder dystocia

There are various techniques for coping with shoulder dystocia. There is no consensus as to which is the best method, that is, the method which allows delivery of the infant with the least amount of damage, but there is consensus that the manoeuvre *not* to undertake is pulling vigorously on the baby's head. This merely pulls the shoulder harder against the pubic bone so delivery cannot occur and the traction exerts a greater lateral force on the neck. As the neck is pulled laterally the nerves coming out of the spine in the neck are stretched. They are rather like a series of guy ropes attached in a descending order on a tent pole. As the tent pole (cervical spine) is pulled laterally, greater tension is exerted on the higher guy ropes (nerve roots) than on the lower. This is why damage occurs in the upper parts of the brachial plexus, C5, 6, (7), first. Thus Erb's palsy, involving the higher roots of the plexus, is more common than Klumpke's palsy, caused by damage to the lower roots, C (7), 8, T1.

The damage to the nerve roots can be via stretching and bruising, when the palsy is temporary or partial, to complete disruption, when the palsy is permanent or semi-permanent. Thus strong traction on the head once shoulder dystocia is diagnosed is no longer acceptable; different techniques must be used and each obstetrics unit must ensure that there is an agreed protocol for coping with shoulder dystocia. Each midwife must be trained and regularly retrained in this agreed method to cope with such an obstetric emergency.

Each of the recognised techniques used attempts to disimpact the anterior shoulder. All techniques can fail, so there needs to be an algorithm detailing the sequence of manoeuvres to be employed to deliver the baby. Delivery of the baby must be effected somehow and, despite utilising an agreed set of manoeuvres, Erb's palsy may occur. Thus Erb's palsy in a child does not necessarily signify a negligent birth; however, the obstetric unit must demonstrate that acceptable techniques were used in an attempt to reduce the chances of a palsy occurring.

Treatment of nerve injuries arising from shoulder dystocia

Treatment of Erb's palsy is physiotherapy, which frequently improves movement. The majority of palsies are temporary, so only a few infants suffer permanent disability. Early operative intervention repairs snapped nerve roots, but is undertaken only in a few specialist centres.

The shoulder joint is inherently unstable. It is a ball-and-socket joint with the end of the humerus resting against the very shallow socket of the shoulder blade. The stability of the joint depends on the ligaments and muscles around the joint. Disruption of the normal muscle tension of the muscles maintaining the shoulder joint, as happens in Erb's palsy, can lead to dislocation of the shoulder joint. Operative intervention is frequently necessary in permanent palsy to stabilise the shoulder joint.

It is impossible to raise the hand to or above the head with a dense nerve palsy. However, children develop tricks to compensate for specific movements, using different muscle groups to effect an action. Thus although the palsy itself may not change, the child's ability may improve over several years, so the eventual disability is not as profound in the older child as in the infant. Any assessment of damages for loss of function should, therefore, be delayed for several years to allow the disability to stabilise.

Treatment of Klumpke's palsy is similar, but the prognosis for recovery is less good than that for Erb's palsy.

Case study: inappropriate delivery techniques for treating shoulder dystocia

Mauricio was Helena's third child; her previous two pregnancies had resulted in live born infants weighing 3.92 kg and 4.38 kg. Helena herself was only 5' 2". The pregnancy with Mauricio was uncomplicated and Helena was booked for a midwife delivery in a GP unit attached to the local hospital. She went into labour at 41 weeks. After some four hours, Mauricio's head was born but his shoulders became stuck. The midwife applied firm traction to the head, to no avail. The midwife then dropped the end of the delivery couch so that Helena's buttocks overhung the end of the couch. The midwife again applied firm traction to Mauricio's head, at the same time shouting to Helena to push down hard; Mauricio remained stuck. Obstetric help was summoned and Mauricio was eventually born after the anterior shoulder had been disimpacted; his collarbone was broken in the process. The Erb's palsy was immediately obvious, so a passive physiotherapy programme was instituted. There was some limited improvement.

His shoulder became dislocated and needed surgical stabilisation. By the age of 10, Mauricio was academically normal, he had some movement at the shoulder and elbow, but little useful function of his fingers. He was independent and could look after his bodily needs, but found co-ordination of finger movement almost impossible, which limited the types of jobs he would be able to undertake in the future.

The claimant argued that the possibility of shoulder dystocia should have been anticipated because of Helena's previous two large babies, and that once the diagnosis of shoulder dystocia had been made it was negligent to try the same procedure, downwards traction, again as this manoeuvre would only worsen the impaction of the shoulder. Whilst it was accepted that an Erb's palsy could occur after shoulder dystocia following any method of delivery, forceful pulling on the head was plainly shown to have the highest rate of this complication. Other accepted second line manoeuvres should have been used.

The defendants argued that shoulder dystocia is unpredictable and is potentially life-threatening. The midwife had managed to deliver Mauricio rapidly in good condition, which was the best outcome, albeit with an Erb's palsy.

The judge did not accept that the possibility of shoulder dystocia should have been anticipated in this case. The debate revolved around the likelihood of shoulder dystocia following delivery by repeated downward traction versus other manoeuvres. The judge found *against* the defendants, arguing that once shoulder dystocia had been diagnosed and there was a failure to deliver the baby with one attempt, then it was medically unacceptable to pursue the same course of action rather than use a recognised manoeuvre for shoulder dystocia. Substantial damages were awarded to the claimants.

Case study: Erb's palsy following multiple attempts at delivery complicated by shoulder dystocia

The midwife suspected shoulder dystocia when there was no restitution (rotation of the head towards the mother's inner thigh) of Dylan's head following delivery. This was confirmed when firm downward traction was exerted on his head. Medical help was summoned. An episiotomy was performed and his mother placed in the MacRobert's position. Delivery was not effected and the lateral position was tried again, unsuccessfully. The obstetric SHO tried to release the posterior shoulder unsuccessfully, and Dylan was eventually delivered after the obstetric registrar was able to disimpact the anterior shoulder, breaking the humerus in the process. Dylan was left with a dense Erb's palsy but was intellectually intact.

The claimants argued that the multiple attempts at delivery had caused the injury, and that once the diagnosis had been confirmed then no further attempts at delivery should have been made until the most experienced available person, the obstetric registrar, could intervene.

The defendants admitted that the Erb's palsy had been caused by shoulder dystocia, but argued that one attempt at normal delivery was necessary for confirmation of the diagnosis. Shoulder dystocia is potentially life-threatening, so it would have been negligent to wait for an unspecified time for the obstetric registrar, who could have been involved in a separate emergency. It was, therefore, appropriate for other professionals, who were appropriately trained, to attempt delivery by accepted methods for shoulder dystocia known to minimise trauma to the infant. All manoeuvres for delivering Dylan were acknowledged as being appropriate in shoulder dystocia and all such manoeuvres carried a risk of causing Erb's palsy. Thus the delivery had been managed appropriately and expediently following the complication of shoulder dystocia, which carried a risk of Erb's palsy.

The judge found for the defendants.

SOFT TISSUE INJURY

Soft tissue injury generally affects the presenting part of the baby. The problems of ventouse extraction and skin loss have been mentioned earlier. Misapplication of forceps can lead to extensive soft tissue damage of the face. However, such damage is commonly only temporary.

The well-being of the fetus before birth is assessed by the cardiotocogram (CTG), which is less reliable during the birth process itself. If there are concerns about the fetus then two methods of assessment are used: fetal blood sampling and direct fetal tracing. Fetal blood sampling involves lacerating the skin over the scalp and collecting the blood so produced. The blade utilised can pierce the skin and fontanelle, causing direct damage to the underlying brain or causing haemorrhage via damage to the underlying venous sinus, for which there can be no excuse.

In direct fetal tracing a scalp electrode is 'screwed' into the skin of the scalp, facilitating electrical contact allowing tracing of the fetal heart rate. The wound so caused normally heals with little problem, and any scar would be covered by hair. Occasionally the area becomes infected, with a commensurately enlarged scar. This of itself does not connote negligence, but inadequate care of the wound, leading to an unnecessarily large scar, would be negligent.

Not infrequently such an electrode is 'screwed' into the buttock, causing scarring. An experienced obstetrician should be able to distinguish between the ends of a fetus.

BONY FRACTURES

Clavicle

The commonest bone to be broken during childbirth is the clavicle, or collarbone. This occurs in approximately two per 1,000 births and is associated with large babies and shoulder dystocia. It is frequently noticed as an incidental finding during the baby's first clinical examination after an apparently normal birth. It is also a recognised complication of shoulder dystocia, so is infrequently the result of negligence.

Humerus

Fracture of the humerus is also a complication of some manoeuvres utilised to overcome shoulder dystocia. Again it is unlikely to have been caused by negligence. It can also occur in breech delivery if the arm is displaced.

Femur

The femur can be fractured in breech deliveries if the legs are extended, that is, when the fetus is 'folded in half' with the legs straight and pointing upwards so the feet are above the head. Manoeuvres to bring down the legs to allow delivery of the baby may result in fractures.

Fractures of the peripheral bones therefore tend to be incidental to the techniques required for delivery of the baby, and infrequently are the result of negligent care.

CHAPTER 3

PERINATAL ASPHYXIA

INTRODUCTION

The financial compensation for children who have been damaged by perinatal asphyxia, or birth asphyxia, is now considerable. As the life expectancy for children with severe learning difficulties increases, the financial provision for their care rises commensurately. There is, therefore, considerable gain to proving perinatal asphyxia by the claimants, and equal gain for disproving it by the defendants. This debate has fuelled the need for there to be an accepted definition of perinatal asphyxia, so that it can be clearly delineated from antenatal insults causing learning difficulties.

DEFINITION OF PERINATAL ASPHYXIA

Despite the many and varied arguments over the subject, there is no unequivocal clinical definition of perinatal asphyxia. The phrase 'perinatal or birth asphyxia' is therefore used quite loosely in the clinical setting and in the clinical notes, as birth asphyxia can be considered as a clinical diagnosis without the rigours required for legal definition. Clinicians may refer to perinatal or birth asphyxia if the baby's Apgar scores were low, regardless of outcome, or it may be inferred in a baby who appears to be suffering from hypoxic ischaemic encephalopathy (HIE), even if the birth was apparently uneventful. Thus such comments in the clinical notes are usually unhelpful. A definition of perinatal asphyxia is, however, germane to the medico-legal argument of causation of neurological damage.

Various authors have attempted to develop a method of defining birth or perinatal asphyxia that satisfies both clinical and legal requirements, though none has gained universal acceptance. Carter *et al* use four questions that require a positive answer for the definition of perinatal asphyxia to be satisfied (see Table 2).

Table 2: Essential characteristics of perinatal asphyxia

1	Profound metabolic or mixed acidosis (pH < 7.00) on an umbilical arterial blood sample.
2	Persistence of an Apgar score of 0 to 3 for > 5 minutes.
3	Clinical neurological sequelae in the immediate neonatal period to include fits, coma or HIE.
4	Evidence of multi-organ failure in the immediate neonatal period.

A low pH indicates increasing acid in the blood, reflecting insufficient oxygenation of the infant. In Chapter 1, arguments were presented to indicate that the five-minute Apgar score was the score most closely associated with outcome. Neurological dysfunction in the form of fits, abnormal behaviour or altered consciousness must be present shortly after birth if there is to be an argument mounted that later neurological damage had its origin in perinatal asphyxia. Multi-organ damage is further evidence of asphyxia, but is less helpful in determining the timing of that asphyxia.

Perlman *et al* have used a similar approach, using several factors (see Table 3). They also looked retrospectively at the requirements for immediate resuscitation. This is helpful in excluding those who are unlikely to have suffered birth asphyxia, but is less helpful in defining those who have definitely suffered birth asphyxia.

Table 3: Conditions required to diagnose perinatal asphyxia

1	No clinical evidence for potential antenatal injury.
2	Absence of antenatal cerebral injury by neuroimaging.
3	Evidence of severe perinatal asphyxia, cord arterial pH < 7.00.
4	Depressed baby requiring intensive resuscitation.
5	Post natal syndrome of HIE.
6	Exclusion of other causes of neonatal encephalopathy.

Neither Carter nor Perlman take into account infants who are partially asphyxiated, have acceptable Apgar scores at birth, do not require aggressive resuscitation, but who do develop later neurological damage.

This lack of agreement has resulted in an internationally accepted position statement that requires a number of criteria to be fulfilled (see Table 4).Unfortunately it is unclear whether, even if all answers are in the affirmative, there can then be no doubt or argument that the infant suffered birth asphyxia. This position statement has not been debated outside the contributing members, so it is unclear whether the medical and legal professions will generally accept it. As well as attempting to define a causal relation between birth asphyxia and subsequent neurological damage, the statement also attempts to alter the terms used. The term 'fetal distress' should no longer be used and should be replaced by the term 'non reassuring fetal status'. 'Birth asphyxia' should similarly be discarded, as the timing of onset of asphyxia is frequently difficult to determine. 'Perinatal asphyxia' should be used, which is much vaguer with regard to timing.

Table 4: Criteria to define an acute intrapartum hypoxic event

	Essential criteria
1	Evidence of a metabolic acidosis in umbilical arterial or very early neonatal blood samples (pH < 7.00 and base deficit ≥ 12mmol/l).
2	Early onset of severe or moderate neonatal encephalopathy in infants of > 34 weeks gestation.
3	Cerebral palsy of the spastic quadriplegic or dyskinetic type.
	Criteria that together suggest an intrapartum timing but by themselves are non-specific
4	A sentinel hypoxic event occurring immediately before or during labour.
5	A sudden, rapid and sustained deterioration of the fetal heart rate pattern usually after the hypoxic sentinel event where the pattern was previously normal.
6	Apgar scores of 0–6 for longer than 5 minutes.
7	Early evidence of multi system involvement.
8	Early imaging evidence of acute cerebral abnormality.

The situation is further complicated if the infant is born prematurely, before 37 completed weeks, as the signs of perinatal asphyxia are different from those in the term baby. This difference becomes greater the more premature the infant is. It is also considerably more difficult to dissect out the contribution of perinatal asphyxia from the multiple other problems that can be suffered by premature infants.

Fetal response to asphyxia

There are different physiological responses to prolonged and acute asphyxia in the term infant; the pre-term infant responds differently again.

If the term infant suffers partial, but relatively prolonged, asphyxia over several hours, the fetus's brain alters its blood flow away from the higher centres of the brain to the mid-brain, which maintains essential bodily functions such as respiration and heart rate. The baby is then born in what appears to be a good condition, with acceptable Apgar scores. The heart rate and respiratory effort are maintained, so no resuscitation may be required. However, as the cerebral hemispheres have been starved of oxygen the baby is likely to demonstrate neurological abnormalities, including hypoxic ischaemic encephalopathy (HIE).

Hypoxic ischaemic encephalopathy

There are three grades of HIE. Grade 1: the infant is irritable, has a high-pitched cry and staring eyes, but is conscious. This grade has a universally good outcome. Grade 2: the infant has fits which start within a few hours of birth; 25% suffer neurological damage. The most serious, grade 3: the child is unconscious and may or may not fit; 50% do not survive; of the remainder, 75% suffer a neurological deficit.

Perinatal asphyxia can be sudden and catastrophic, such as in abruption of the placenta, depriving the fetus of oxygen. There is no time for the adaptive measures in blood flow to maintain the vital mid-brain centres. The fetus is born with low Apgar scores, poor heart rate and respiratory effort, requiring resuscitation. It is likely that the infant will suffer HIE. Such babies fulfil the Carter criteria.

Neuro-imaging in asphyxia

Magnetic resonance imaging (MRI) of the head will show permanent damage to the cerebral hemispheres, but an intact mid-brain and basal ganglia (vital centres) in chronic partial asphyxia. In acute asphyxia, both the cerebral hemispheres and basal ganglia are damaged. Later MRI is thus helpful to determine the type of asphyxia suffered, but cannot be used to determine the precise timing of that asphyxia. The two types of asphyxia could have occurred antenatally or perinatally.

The picture is more complicated in the pre-term infant. The pre-term brain does not have the ability to alter or preserve blood flow during times of insult. The main arteries to the brain have circumscribed areas of distribution, and the regions at the periphery of these have relatively poor blood supply and so are vulnerable to oxygen starvation. Perinatal asphyxia in the pre-term infant leads to damage around the cerebral ventricles, which are in the centre of the brain.

The damaged brain tissue is then slowly re-absorbed, so by about 10 days after the insult a cyst can be seen developing: periventricular leukomalacia. The appearance of such cysts approximately dates the time of the asphyxia. It is, therefore, important to undertake ultrasound scans of the head in pre-term infants from shortly after birth.

Outcome of perinatal asphyxia

Outcome is virtually impossible to predict in the neonatal period in moderate or severe hypoxia. There are some children who were born clinically dead, that is, their Apgar scores were 0 at birth. However, resuscitation produced a heart rate and respiratory effort and the baby eventually lived. Some of these children will be developmentally and intellectually normal, others will have moderate or severe learning difficulties. It may be that the determining factor for outcome is the length of time of the asphyxia, which is normally impossible to determine as few babies are monitored in the second stage of labour.

Babies who appear normal at birth and then develop HIE have a similar range of outcomes. Although the statistical neurological outcomes for different grades of HIE are known, they are not helpful for individual babies.

The outcome, therefore, for individual babies only becomes determinable with assessment of development over a protracted period of time. Infants may appear to be developing normally, begin to sit or crawl or walk at the appropriate times, but when schooling starts it becomes obvious that there is a deficit in higher functions. It is of great importance, therefore, when considering whether an episode of perinatal asphyxia has had a lasting effect that the developmental and intellectual status of the child is assessed after a period of schooling.

Case study: perinatal asphyxia with a poor outcome

Arabella's mother, a primipara, went into what she thought was normal term labour. She self-referred herself to her obstetrics unit where she had received appropriate antenatal care for a first pregnancy. Her hand-held obstetric record showed no complications of pregnancy, blood pressure was normal and the kick chart (number of fetal movements felt in 24 hours) was completed. The obstetric unit was busy; she was rapidly assessed as being in early labour and placed on a trolley in the corridor outside the labour ward. She was seen intermittently by midwives, who listened to the fetal heart with a fetal stethoscope. No continuous monitoring (cardiotocogram (CTG)) was applied. Five hours later, when she was moved into the labour ward, a CTG was commenced which was grossly abnormal and she underwent an emergency caesarean section. Arabella needed aggressive resuscitation at birth, suffered fits and eventually developed cerebral palsy. The claimant argued that, had she been properly assessed and monitored, abnormalities in the CTG would have been noticed earlier, with a resultant earlier delivery. It would have been likely that Arabella would have had a normal outcome had she been delivered promptly when CTG abnormalities could have been first noticed.

The defendants argued that the unit was extraordinarily busy and that they gave the best obstetric care possible in the circumstances. There was no disagreement as to the causation of Arabella's cerebral palsy.

The judge ruled that the NHS had a duty of care to its patients and that a lesser quality of care could not be accepted. If a unit has insufficient staff for the number of patients, then extra nurses or doctors should be drafted in or patients moved to other units. The case was decided in the claimant's favour.

ANTENATAL ASPHYXIA

The preference for using the term 'perinatal asphyxia' as opposed to 'birth asphyxia' relates to the recognition that a fetus can suffer asphyxia in the womb from which it can recover, so is apparently normal at birth. It is only later that brain damage becomes obvious as the infant demonstrates learning difficulties. The type of asphyxia is likely to have been either dramatic but very short lasting, or partial and more prolonged. The timing of such asphyxia is usually unknown; however, if there has been continuous CTG monitoring then on occasion a period of abnormal CTG may be detectable. There is increasing evidence that antenatal events, rather than birth asphyxia, are the cause of the majority, possibly 80% or 90%, of cases of cerebral palsy.

It had been thought that birth asphyxia or birth damage was the main cause of later problems such as cerebral palsy. However, over the past 20 years obstetric care has improved considerably, but there has not been a commensurate decrease in the incidence of cerebral palsy. Thus, although there are still instances of obvious birth asphyxia causing brain damage, the majority of children with learning difficulties have, in retrospect, had an entirely normal and uneventful birth. Antenatal events, either inherent in the fetus or secondary to maternal or intrauterine problems, constitute the major cause of learning difficulties in children.

Case study: possible antenatal asphyxia causing cerebral palsy

Charlotte was Elsie's third child. Elsie's waters broke at 39 weeks' gestation after an uncomplicated pregnancy and she self-referred to her normal maternity unit. CTG was commenced which showed a normal fetal trace. Over the next eight hours intermittent CTGs were considered acceptable, and Charlotte was delivered in good condition. She breast-fed well and mother and daughter were discharged at 48 hours.

At the six-week follow-up, it was noticed that Charlotte was not smiling and over the next few months it became obvious that she was significantly delayed. Extensive investigation included an MRI scan that showed an intact mid-brain but damaged cerebral hemispheres, consistent with partial prolonged asphyxia. Review of the CTGs revealed abnormalities in the trace taken some six hours before delivery, with resolution of the abnormalities approximately 40 minutes later.

The claimants argued that the attending midwife was negligent in failing to interpret the CTG correctly and had she done so, an emergency caesarean section would have been undertaken. Charlotte would then not have been so damaged and may have been developmentally normal.

The defendants argued that it was impossible to stipulate categorically that the 40 minutes' abnormality had caused Charlotte problems, and further, that the changes noted on the trace could indicate problems other than asphyxia. Also, even if they had acted on the CTG it would have taken approximately 30 minutes to deliver Charlotte, saving at most 10 minutes. If the particular episode had been the exclusive cause of Charlotte's present problems, then it was likely that the reduction of asphyxia by 10 minutes would have made little difference to the outcome.

The judge found for the defendants, stating that it was impossible to be sure that the CTG changes only indicated asphyxia, and that if Charlotte had suffered one episode of unexplained asphyxia she could have suffered others that were not noted because of intermittent monitoring. Thus Charlotte may well have been damaged before the noted CTG changes. Further, even if there was only one episode of asphyxia it was unlikely that much of the asphyxia period would have been shortened by caesarean section, so the outcome would have been no different.

References

Carter, BS, Haverkamp, D and Merenstein, GB, 'The definition of acute perinatal asphyxia' (1993) 20 Clinics in Perinatology 287–304.

MacLennan, A, 'A template for defining a causal relation between acute intrapartum events and cerebral palsy: international consensus statement' (1999) 319 BMJ 1054–59.

Perlman, JM, 'Intrapartum hypoxic-ischaemic cerebral injury and subsequent cerebral palsy: medico-legal issues' (1997) 99 Pediatrics 851–59.

CHAPTER 4

LEARNING DIFFICULTIES

INTRODUCTION

Accepted teaching for the majority of this century indicated that the cause of the cerebral palsy was birth asphyxia. However, obstetric practice has steadily improved, but there has not been a concomitant reduction in the incidence of cerebral palsy in term infants. In addition, retrospective analysis of the perinatal events in children with cerebral palsy has demonstrated that very few, possibly only 10–20%, suffered perinatal compromise that may have been a contributory factor to the subsequent cerebral palsy. It has thus become increasingly clear that birth asphyxia is the cause of relatively few cases of cerebral palsy, and antenatal factors or events probably cause the majority of cases.

The question that must, therefore, be asked is: how much of cerebral palsy is caused by birth asphyxia and how much has birth asphyxia in any particular case contributed to cerebral palsy?

ANTENATAL ANTECEDENTS OF CEREBRAL PALSY

The majority of children who are diagnosed as having cerebral palsy have had what appears to have been a trouble-free pregnancy, birth and neonatal period. The slow realisation that development is not occurring at the normal pace is most painful for parents, the pain compounded by the lack of answers as to why.

Retrospective studies have attempted to delineate the causes of, or at least the antenatal associations with, cerebral palsy. The most obvious association is between prematurity and cerebral palsy. However, great difficulty can be encountered when attempting to separate out the cause of the premature birth itself, which may also have had a compromising effect on the fetus *in utero*, the acute trauma of birth on a potentially compromised fetus, and the postnatal difficulties frequently experienced by such pre-term infants. The remainder of this chapter, therefore, assumes an infant born at term, greater than or equal to 37 weeks' gestation, unless otherwise stipulated.

Small for gestational age (SGA)

The term 'small for gestational age' (SGA) indicates a birth weight of less than the 10th centile for infants of that gestation, that is, the lightest 10% of all babies. The cause of an infant being small is frequently not known. Some fetuses are genetically small and thus normally and healthily fall within this bottom 10%; however, others are not. There are two broad categories of SGA babies: proportionate and disproportionate. The proportionate babies are just that: their length, weight and head circumference are proportionate. These babies may be those genetically small but normal; others may have suffered from intra-uterine malnutrition for some considerable time during pregnancy and have, therefore, been unable to grow to their full potential. This latter group has suffered chronic intra-uterine compromise.

It is thought that the disproportionate SGA babies have suffered a shorter time of intra-uterine compromise. They have the same head circumference and length of their plumper soul mates, but are thin and scrawny, lacking in subcutaneous fat. They are SGA by virtue of being thin but not short. It is easy, therefore, to spot the disproportionate SGA, but somewhat more difficult to differentiate between the proportionate SGA and the small normal baby.

There is a strong association between SGA and cerebral palsy. Part of the association may relate to the same antenatal insult causing both the SGA and cerebral palsy. Another aspect could be the reduced ability of a compromised SGA fetus to withstand the rigours of labour without damage.

Congenital abnormalities

Congenital abnormalities, neurological and non-neurological, have been consistently associated with cerebral palsy independent of being SGA, even though there is a close association between congenital malformations and SGA. These congenital malformations may be part of an obvious syndrome of which part is cerebral palsy, or there may be more subtle neurological abnormalities, such as the abnormal migration of brain cells during organ development. Even if these neurological abnormalities do not directly cause cerebral palsy, there is again a strong association between neurological disorders and cerebral palsy. These various combinations and permutations argue strongly for MRI scanning of the brain in an attempt to define the underlying disorder.

Oxygen delivery to the fetus

The fetus is entirely dependent on maternal/placental blood flow for intact survival. The placenta embeds in the wall of the womb and virtually covers a lake of maternal blood. The fetal circulation is separate from that of the mother, so exchange of oxygen and nutrients occurs from this maternal lake of blood across the walls of the small fetal blood vessels of the placenta. If the placenta becomes separated from the maternal blood supply (placental abruption), the fetus is at risk of hypoxic damage. This is the mechanism for fetal neurological damage with ante-partum haemorrhage. The placenta comes away from the wall of the womb, allowing the mother to haemorrhage, but also compromising oxygen supply to be fetus. Although the fetal circulation is separate the fetal blood vessels can be damaged, leading to fetal haemorrhage as well, which will further compromise the fetus. Such a haemorrhage may be obvious, causing vaginal bleeding; however, the placenta may break away from the womb, but contain the resulting haemorrhage. The maternal blood lake therefore enlarges, becomes relatively stagnant, and clots, causing compromise to the fetus that can range from intra-uterine death to neurological damage. This placental abruption may have happened some time before birth, so that the baby is born in what appears to be good condition. The retroplacental clot may not be looked for or recognised, thus the cause of later cerebral palsy is missed.

Intra-uterine infections

The fetus develops in a sterile environment and the placenta also acts as a barrier to protect the fetus. However, certain drugs and infections can cross from the mother to the fetus, causing damage during development which can affect neurological development.

The common infections that can cross the placenta are rubella (german measles), toxoplasmosis gondii (toxoplasma: a single cell organism), *Cytomegalovirus* and *Listeria*. Rubella infection is now rare, because of the infant immunisation programme which protects the growing girl and thus the adult pregnant woman from contracting rubella. Toxoplasmosis can be acquired from undercooked meat, especially undercooked lamb, so is not a problem if meat is properly cooked. *Listeria* can be acquired from cold food, such as soft cheese. Public health advice concerning foodstuffs during pregnancy is aimed at reducing the chances of mothers acquiring such infections.

Cytomegalovirus is endemic in our society. It may cause a mild illness similar to glandular fever, but frequently the mother is infected silently with no adverse effects; the fetus, though, may be damaged. Fortunately, because the virus is endemic, many children and adolescents contract the virus and so are immune to it before pregnancy.

The features of early intra-uterine infection are usually obvious at birth. The baby will have microcephaly (small head), may well be SGA, and may have damaged eyes. Diagnosis should not be difficult.

Antenatal cerebro-vascular accidents

Abnormal events in cerebral circulation may also cause neurological damage. Intra-uterine strokes have been described which cause cell death in the brain. The damaged area is re-absorbed, leaving a fluid filled hole (porencephalic cyst), usually communicating with the ventricular system of the brain.

Intra-uterine cerebral trauma

Amniocentesis is undertaken for various obstetric indications. A needle is passed through the mother's abdomen and into the womb under ultrasound guidance and some amniotic fluid removed for analysis. Ultrasound guidance is important to locate the fetus and the liquor pools. Occasionally, the amniocentesis needle can pierce the fetus, including the head, causing direct trauma.

The fetus can, therefore, suffer a multiplicity of antenatal insults, acute or chronic, which can lay the foundations for later cerebral palsy.

PERINATAL FACTORS

The considerable contribution of perinatal asphyxia to the development of learning difficulties has been discussed in Chapter 3.

PREMATURITY AND CEREBRAL PALSY

Prematurity is the greatest risk factor for cerebral palsy. Antenatal problems, as discussed above, may be a cause of premature labour or compromise of the fetus. The birth process is traumatic and is increasingly so the more premature the delivery. Postnatal problems also increase in severity the greater the prematurity; it is suggested that 35–40% of children with cerebral palsy were born prematurely. The pre-term infant's brain may suffer damage during the birth process, especially if born in the breech position. After birth the pre-term infant may suffer spontaneous intraventricular haemorrhage (bleeding into the centre of the brain); have immature lungs, making oxygen supply difficult; or the heart may not be able to maintain an adequate blood pressure. All of these factors can compromise the delivery of oxygen to the brain, so causing damage. Thus it is often difficult, if not impossible, to win a causation argument in a case involving a pre-term infant with many postnatal difficulties, even if obstetric negligence is proven.

Case study: defective equipment causing cerebral palsy in an otherwise normal pre-term infant

Tina was born at 28 weeks' gestation in a maternity unit that only had special care baby facilities. She developed moderately severe respiratory distress and required intubation and ventilation. Arrangements were made to transfer her to a neonatal intensive care unit in the nearby city some 45 minutes away. Tina was stabilised initially on the ventilator, intravenous access was established and an umbilical arterial catheter sited. Tina's vital signs were stable, she was then transferred to the transport incubator and ventilator and was stabilised before the transfer journey began. Unfortunately the oxygen supply for the transport ventilator ran out some 15 minutes before arriving at the neonatal intensive care unit, so she was ventilated with air only. When Tina arrived on the neonatal unit her heart had stopped. She was successfully resuscitated but subsequently developed spastic quadriplegic cerebral palsy.

The claimants argued that no one had checked the oxygen level in the oxygen cylinder before departure, and anyway back-up supplies should be carried. The defendants admitted liability with regard to oxygen supply but argued that Tina was at risk of developing cerebral palsy anyway because of her gestational age.

The claimants argued that Tina did not suffer any intra-cranial insult, such as a haemorrhage, either at the referring hospital or after she had been resuscitated, and an uncomplicated infant born at 28 weeks' gestation is not at high risk of developing cerebral palsy. The only insult she had suffered, therefore, was a cardiac arrest directly attributable to the lack of oxygen in the ambulance. The claim was settled out of court for a substantial sum.

Case study: lack of oxygen to the brain and subsequent neonatal stroke

Bradley was born following a crash caesarean section when the scalp blood sample indicated severe fetal acidosis. Despite prompt action by the obstetric staff Bradley was effectively born dead, with Apgar scores of 0 at one minute. He was intubated, cardiac massage instituted and adrenaline administered. He was rapidly resuscitated, regaining a normal heart rate by five minutes of life. He was transferred to the neonatal unit stabilised on a ventilator, arterial and venous access established. His blood pressure initially was low, but remained stable after receiving extra fluids.

A cranial ultrasound scan on the first day of life was reported as normal. He progressed rapidly and came off the ventilator on day two of life. A repeat cranial ultrasound on day three was similarly reported as normal, but a further scan on day four demonstrated a haemorrhage within the brain tissue. This area of haemorrhage was eventually re-absorbed, leaving Bradley with a porencephalic cyst.

Developmental follow-up demonstrated that Bradley had moderate learning difficulties, although little in the way of physical handicap.

A review of the obstetric care of the labour indicated that the CTGs were sufficiently abnormal for Bradley to have been born some three hours earlier. This was accepted by the defendants. There was, however, disagreement as to causation.

The claimants argued that the perinatal asphyxia that Bradley must have suffered because of his cardiac arrest caused damage to the fetal brain. There was, then, the potential for there to be a haemorrhage into that damaged brain tissue. Bradley did not suffer from an intra-ventricular haemorrhage, which is a recognised risk in a pre-term infant. As Bradley, at the time of the haemorrhage, was in a stable condition there were therefore no risk factors for haemorrhage. The defendants argued that haemorrhagic infarction occurs spontaneously and that the events surrounding birth were no longer relevant by the fourth day.

The experts from the two sides could not agree. There is no evidence to suggest a correlation between low Apgar scores at birth and subsequent intra-cerebral haemorrhage. The area of haemorrhage was such that it could have been caused by an infarction or from spontaneous haemorrhage into a damaged and softened area of the brain.

The judge found for the claimants. Bradley had without doubt suffered perinatal asphyxia. At his gestation there are 'watershed' areas of the brain with poor arterial supply, which lie between the boundaries of the areas supplied by the major cerebral arteries. These 'watershed' areas are at risk of damage during a period of low blood pressure or blood flow that happens when the heart stops beating. These damaged areas soften several days after birth, which could allow subsequent haemorrhage. Cerebral infarction occurs but is uncommon, therefore in Bradley's case, on the balance of probabilities, perinatal asphyxia followed by brain cell death and subsequent haemorrhage into the damaged area was the most likely cause of his subsequent learning difficulties.

OXYGEN DELIVERY TO THE BRAIN AFTER BIRTH

Postnatal cerebro-vascular accidents

The term infant, if born in good condition with normal developmental potential, generally suffers little in the way of postnatal insults. Spontaneous stroke involving one of the major brain blood vessels, usually the middle cerebral artery, will cause extensive brain damage, but as it is spontaneous is of no medico-legal significance. Postnatal brain damage in the term infant is more commonly secondary to oxygen starvation, either from lung damage or from inadequate circulation, rather than from intra-cranial events.

Meconium (fetal stool) aspiration

The post-term infant, 41–42 weeks, may pass meconium (fetal stool) normally, as the intestines should be working. The term infant may also pass meconium, but is more likely to do so if in distress. If meconium is passed in the womb and the fetus is undertaking breathing movements, meconium can be taken into the lungs. This acts as a mechanical block to gas exchange, with plugs of meconium blocking the lung airways. It also acts as a chemical irritant, destroying surfactant, the chemical lining of the lungs, which is vital for normal lung action. These two mechanisms can dramatically reduce the ability of the lungs to transfer oxygen, so indirectly causing brain damage.

Medico-legal claims would revolve around the conduct of the birth and whether there was adequate warning that the baby was distressed, as well as around the quality of neonatal care. If thick meconium is present during the birth, a paediatrician should attend to attempt to suck out any meconium in the baby's mouth, and also to visualise the vocal cords and to suck out any visible meconium around or below the vocal cords. Although this may be helpful, it may not prevent meconium aspiration. Thus the medico-legal discussions would revolve around adequate and appropriate care of the complications of the aspiration.

Persistent fetal circulation

The default fetal circulation is to divert blood away from the lungs, which are of no relevance *in utero*. The infant circulation is inherently unstable in the first few days of life, so if the lungs are compromised, for example, by meconium aspiration, the infant's circulation may revert to that of the fetus, with blood being diverted away from the lungs, reducing oxygen supply to the brain. The reversion to fetal circulation is spontaneous and may be unavoidable. Again, the medico-legal arguments revolve around the quality of treatment for reversal of the fetal circulation rather than whether or not it could have been prevented.

It is clear, therefore, that ante-, peri- and postnatal insults can all cause the subsequent cerebral palsy.

JAUNDICE/KERNICTERUS

The infant liver is relatively immature and may not be able to cope with levels of jaundice produced by the baby in the first few days of life. This is more so the more premature the baby. If the levels of jaundice become very high (this level depends on the prematurity of the baby), then certain structures in the brain, the basal ganglia, are damaged. These structures are important in the control of movement; damage can therefore cause abnormal movements: athetosis and chorea. Athetosis describes uncontrolled slow writhing movements of the limbs; chorea, jerky movements.

CEREBRAL PALSY

Definition

Cerebral palsy is the result of an insult to the fetal brain as described above. The insult or injury itself does not change; however, because of the natural growth and development of the child the physical manifestation of the neurological damage may change. It is therefore a non-progressive, chronic disability that results in abnormal control of movement and posture.

There is one postnatal insult which causes a predictable type of cerebral palsy: kernicterus leads to athetoid cerebral palsy with high tone deafness. The outcome of other perinatal insults are more difficult to predict.

There are three broad categories of cerebral palsy: spastic, dyskinetic and ataxic.

Spastic cerebral palsy

Spasticity means muscle stiffness, so it is very difficult to move the voluntary muscles. Voluntary muscles are those that we have control over, such as the muscles in the limbs, but also the tongue and muscles around the voice box. Children who are most severely affected with spastic cerebral palsy, therefore, not only have difficulty with movements but also difficulty with speaking, chewing and swallowing their food.

Spastic quadriplegia

This is the most severe form of spastic cerebral palsy. All four limbs are affected, with the arms more affected than the legs, as well as the muscles for chewing and speech. The child usually has severe learning difficulty so is unable to communicate, mainly because of the severe learning difficulty but also because of muscle problems in the voice box. These children frequently cannot sit up or walk independently and are not able to achieve independent existence. They require constant care and attention for all their bodily requirements; this need persists throughout their natural life. Perinatal asphyxia is the cause of a few such cases, but the majority are caused by antenatal insults as described above.

Spastic hemiplegia

Hemiplegia refers to one side of the body being affected, that is, the arm and leg on the same side. The arm is normally more severely affected than the leg. Thus the children are able to walk, albeit not with an easy gait, but the arm and hand often have restricted use. The fingers may be permanently in the shape of a fist, and it is often difficult to relax the fingers so that fine movement of that hand is severely compromised.

The Consensus Statement (see Chapter 3), which attempts to define the relationship between perinatal asphyxia and cerebral palsy, contains a categorical statement that hemiplegia is not caused by perinatal asphyxia. The underlying causes are likely to be brain malformations, strokes or prenatal haemorrhage into the brain tissue. MRI or CT scanning may be able to give a precise cause, so giving relief to parents and obstetricians alike.

Spastic diplegia

All four limbs are affected, but with the lower limbs being considerably more affected than the upper limbs. The arms, hands and fingers may be mildly affected, allowing normal hand and arm movements. The lower limbs, however, are stiff and difficult to move. Such children may be able to walk without walking aids but their gait is rather jerky and sometimes unstable. Their intelligence is usually unaffected, so they follow the normal childhood developmental pattern and achieve independent existence.

Dyskinetic cerebral palsy

Dyskinetic cerebral palsy includes involuntary movements affecting all four limbs, the face, the voice box and the trunk. The abnormal movements come from damage to structures in the brain called basal ganglia: these are the structures damaged by kernicterus. These children are constantly moving involuntarily, so voluntary movements are either difficult or impossible. It is very difficult for these children to talk, as the muscles around the voice box cannot be easily controlled. Similarly they may have difficulties with chewing and swallowing. These children may, however, have normal intelligence but have to suffer the frustration of not being able to communicate unless they have access to electronic devices that aid communication.

Athetoid cerebral palsy

Athetoid movements are slow, purposeless movements, and they may be referred to as writhing. Athetoid cerebral palsy, with no added jerking choreiform movements, is now almost always due to perinatal asphyxia, as kernicterus is uncommon.

Choreiform cerebral palsy

Again, these movements are purposeless but are short-lived twitching movements; they may be incorporated into voluntary movements to hide them.

Ataxic cerebral palsy

These are characterised by lack of muscle power (floppiness or hypotonia), difficulty in co-ordinating purposeful voluntary movements, and difficulty with balance.

Despite these broad classifications, there are some children who display mixed patterns but who undeniably are suffering from cerebral palsy.

LIFE EXPECTANCY

Life expectancy in children with learning difficulties and/or cerebral palsy is very difficult to predict. There have been many studies attempting to utilise particular categories of disability in order to improve life prediction, which are helpful. However, life expectancy is improving constantly so estimates need to be reviewed and revised frequently.

Methods have been devised which use particular categories, relating to severity of disability, in order to provide a risk factor to be used against normal life expectancy. The most important areas for life prediction appear to be those concerned with mobility and feeding ability.

The study by Hutton *et al* in 1994 found that manual dexterity and ambulatory ability were good predictors of survival. Although they started with four categories for manual dexterity, they found that three could be amalgamated into a mild group: this group ranged from having their upper limbs unaffected to being able to feed and dress with difficulty; and a severe group, not able to feed and dress independently. Those with a mild disability had a 97% chance of reaching the age of 20; those with severe disability had a 55% chance.

Similar figures were found for ambulatory ability. Mild disability ranged from being able to run and climb stairs, but with less ability than those unaffected, through to wheelchair-bound children who could propel themselves: these had a 98% chance survival to the age of 20. Those severely affected, that is, needing a wheelchair and also assistance to push it, had a 56% chance of reaching the age of 20.

The level of IQ was less helpful: those with an IQ of less than 50 had a 73% chance of survival to the age of 20, as opposed to a 98% chance for children with an IQ greater than 50.

A later paper by Strauss used two main categories: mobility and the ability to feed. Instead of indicating percentage survival, shown in the Hutton paper, the study calculates a 'hazard ratio', that is, likelihood of death. For example, the child who is unable to lift his head when lying on his back is eight times more likely to die in a given year than a child who has some independent mobility. Even a child who is able to lift his head but not chest has a sixfold increase in chances of death as compared to an ambulatory child.

Those children who are tube-fed, that is, do not have sufficient oral skills to swallow food or fluid, have a fivefold increase in their chances of dying as compared with children who can feed by mouth.

Interestingly, both papers indicate that the presence of cerebral palsy increases the risk of death only modestly. However, the prediction curve for survival of the most severely affected children (children unable to lift their heads, lacking hand use, with spastic quadriplegia and severe learning difficulties) have a median survival of 11.8 years. The most severely affected children, therefore, still have a relatively short life span; as disability lessens, length of survival time is virtually the same as the general population. The range of life expectancy is considerable, so prediction requires access to the latest studies as well as the possession of the appropriate clinical skills.

References

Hutton, JL, Cooke, T and Pharoah, POD, 'Life expectancy in children with cerebral palsy' (1994) 309 BMJ 431–35.

Strauss, DJ, Shavelle, RM and Anderson, TW, 'Life expectancy of children with cerebral palsy' (1998) 18 Pediatr Neurol 143–49.

CHAPTER 5

NEONATAL CARE

INTRODUCTION

The new-born baby has just survived the ordeal of birth. However, it is relatively ill-equipped for independent life and has to overcome many potential hurdles to survive. This chapter describes several disparate problems that may assault such a babe.

VITAMIN K DEFICIENCY

Vitamin K is vital for the production of several blood clotting factors made by the liver. Deficiency or insufficiency of vitamin K in new-born babies can lead to haemorrhage: haemorrhagic disease of the new-born. This can be spontaneous but harmless, for example, resulting in bleeding from the umbilical stump (the tummy button) when the umbilical cord falls off around 10–14 days. However, if bleeding occurs in the head this is potentially extremely serious. Most babies who have thus suffered have either died or been left with major neurological damage.

Diagnosis

Diagnosis of haemorrhagic disease of the new-born is based on clinical suspicion confirmed by laboratory testing of the baby's blood clotting system. There are two pathways involved in blood clotting and different factors are involved in these pathways. The laboratory results differentiate between the pathways and imply which blood factors are deficient, allowing a precise diagnosis to be made.

Treatment

Treatment is to correct the clotting abnormality quickly by giving clotting factors and also by giving vitamin K.

Prevention

Formula, or bottle-fed, infants are not very likely to suffer from vitamin K deficiency as baby milk is fortified with vitamin K; exclusively breast-fed babies are the group who potentially have deficiency as there is not much vitamin K in breast milk. During the mid-1980s a mini epidemic of haemorrhagic disease of the new-born was reported. Previously many maternity units had given intramuscular injections of vitamin K to high-risk infants, considered to be breast-fed and premature infants. Following the report from Exeter the majority of maternity units gave vitamin K to all babies regardless of gestational age or feeding type. This led to a dramatic decrease in the reported cases of haemorrhagic disease of the new-born.

In the early 1990s a highly publicised report suggested that intramuscular vitamin K was associated with an increased incidence of childhood malignancy. This caused widespread consternation amongst parents and the medical profession. The report was examined in minute detail and repeated in several other countries. The association between vitamin K and childhood malignancy has not been proven. In the meantime, some maternity units only offered oral vitamin K, some gave the parents a choice, and some continued with the intramuscular form. At present there is no consensus as to the appropriate method of administering vitamin K, and the above options can be found being promulgated around the UK. One dose of the intramuscular vitamin K is sufficient to prevent haemorrhagic disease of the new-born, but three separate doses of the oral preparation are necessary for prevention. As there are concerns about compliance with the three oral doses versus the one intramuscular, there is still debate as to the safest vitamin K prophylaxis. However, each maternity or neonatal unit should have a clear written protocol detailing the preferred method in that unit, and how the unit reacts to high-risk groups and to those few parents who decline any form of vitamin K whatever. In my own unit we have a policy of only offering intramuscular vitamin K as a first line treatment, with the dose, date and time of administration clearly documented. If parents object, a junior doctor gives them advice as to the merits and demerits of intramuscular and oral vitamin K. If oral vitamin K is preferred then this is prescribed with a letter to the GP to prescribe the second and third doses. Some parents refuse vitamin K completely. A consultant paediatrician, who will rehearse the arguments for vitamin K, sees them. If refusal continues, this is clearly documented in the notes along with the parental reasons if possible. Fortunately, haemorrhagic disease is still unusual even in exclusively breast-fed babies given no extra vitamin K. After all, generations of infants have been exclusively breast-fed until the beginning of the last century and happily survived.

Case study: wrong advice concerning vitamin K causing neurological damage

Dino was the first-born child of Malaysian parents. They were seen by a consultant paediatrician who noted that Dino's mother wished to breast feed, but told the parents that Dino did not need vitamin K, as it wasn't necessary for babies of Far Eastern extraction.

Twelve days later, Dino's parents noted that there was blood in his mouth. They cleaned his mouth, but noticed that his gums were bleeding. He then had a fit. They rushed him to hospital, where it was clear that his blood clotting was grossly deranged and that he had suffered a bleed into his head. His blood clotting was corrected and he survived, but with severe neurological damage. At the age of four years, it was apparent that Dino's development was severely compromised and his parents sought legal advice, arguing that they had been given the wrong advice concerning the necessity for Dino to have vitamin K. If they had been given the correct advice they would have allowed Dino to receive the vitamin K, which would have prevented any bleeding.

The defence reiterated the advice given about vitamin K in different ethnic groups, but failed to produce a unit policy on the use of vitamin K. The medical advice was easily proven to be wrong, and the lack of a policy for vitamin K administration was considered to be negligent. Substantial damages were agreed out of court.

PERINATAL INFECTIONS

Herpes and other viral infections

Fetuses and babies are prone to infection because their immune systems are relatively immature. The three main causes of infection of the fetus in the womb are rubella (german measles), toxoplasmosis and *Cytomegalovirus*. The effect that these infections have on the fetus depends on the timing of the infection during gestation. If infection occurs in the early stages (first trimester) when the organs are developing, considerable damage to the fetus can occur, with significant injury to the brain. The major reason for the rubella vaccination is to reduce the chances of rubella damage to the fetus. Little can be done to reduce the infection rate of toxoplasmosis and CMV apart from dietary advice, for example, not eating rare cooked lamb that can harbour toxoplasmosis.

Diagnosis

Genital herpes is a sexually transmitted disease that can produce obvious lesions on the external genitalia, but can also remain within the internal genitalia causing a hidden infection of the cervix (neck of the womb). New-born babies resist an infection with herpes poorly. The virus becomes widespread and overwhelming, causing a severe infection that may be fatal even with treatment. It is recommended, therefore, that babies should be born by elective caesarean section if there is concern about active genital herpes in the mother. There may be no knowledge of the mother's herpetic state, so the possibility of a viral infection with herpes is frequently considered in babies who are clinically infected, but in whom no focus of the infection is found. A skin rash of vesicles (fluid filled blisters) should raise the possibility of herpes.

Treatment

The treatment for herpes, the drug acyclovir, is relatively harmless compared to the potential severity of untreated herpes, so there should be a low threshold for instigating anti-herpes treatment if there is any possibility of such an infection.

Case study: dormant genital herpes leading to infection of the baby

Dale was 22 year old Lisa's first baby. She was known to have had genital herpes when she was 18 years old, but there was no evidence of active herpes either on her external or internal genitalia during this pregnancy. A decision was made for vaginal delivery; however, Lisa developed pre-eclampsia (high blood pressure, ankle swelling and protein in the urine) so Dale was delivered by elective caesarean section at 39 weeks' gestation in a maternity unit with special baby care facilities only. Lisa had neither gone into spontaneous labour nor had her membranes ruptured before section.

Dale went back to the postnatal ward with his mother and enjoyed his first feed. However, over the next few hours he became lethargic and wouldn't feed. He was seen by the paediatricians, who were concerned that he might be infected. He was admitted to the baby unit and given antibiotics and intravenous fluids. Dale's blood clotting was deranged, he had evidence of liver damage and he had abnormally high levels of acid in his blood. The paediatricians were unsure of the overall diagnosis, so asked for a second opinion from the nearby intensive care baby unit. The paediatrician from that unit reviewed Dale a few hours later. He considered several possible diagnoses, including herpes infection, but decided that the most likely cause was an inborn error of metabolism: an inability to cope with the breakdown products of food. Further investigations were sent off, including those for herpes, and treatment instituted to correct Dale's various problems. Despite intensive care Dale worsened and he died, aged two days. The following day the herpes test came back positive.

The claimants argued that Dale should have been treated for herpes immediately there was a concern about infection. All of the abnormalities found, the blood clotting, liver damage and acid levels, could be explained by herpes, so nothing would have been lost by treating for herpes even if that diagnosis had proved wrong eventually. If anti-herpes treatment had been started at the same time as the antibiotics then Dale would have made a complete recovery.

The defendants argued that the problem of herpes had been anticipated. Lisa had been examined and no active lesions found, and anyway Dale had been delivered before Lisa's membranes had broken, by caesarean section. There were, therefore, no risk factors for herpes. The paediatrician giving the second opinion had considered herpes, but had felt it was an unlikely diagnosis given the mode of delivery. All of Dale's problems could also have been explained by an inborn error of metabolism.

The case was decided for the defendants, on the grounds that there were no risk factors for herpes infection, the paediatrician had considered the diagnosis so was not negligent in ignoring the possibility, and that, on the balance of probabilities, herpes was not likely to have been the diagnosis. It was successfully argued that the clinical judgment of the paediatrician not to treat for herpes 'just in case' would have been supported by a reasonable number of paediatricians.

Streptococcal and other bacterial infections

Group B *Streptococcus* infection of the new-born may have a similarly fatal outcome to viral infections as above. Group B *Streptococcus* is present in the vagina of some 15–20% of women and is considered to be sexually transmitted. During birth the baby may be colonised by the bacterium that is present harmlessly on the skin. Occasionally the organism becomes invasive, causing a serious and potentially fatal infection. Infants who have had an instrumental birth, that is, by forceps or Ventouse extraction, causing breaches in the skin, and premature infants are at higher risk of being infected than normal term infants. The organism may also infect the fetus still in the womb. The liquor becomes infected and the *Streptococcus* enters the lungs via the normal breathing movements of the fetus, causing pneumonia. This is more likely if the membranes have been ruptured for several hours. From the pneumonia, septicaemia can develop.

Prevention

Attempts have been made to eradicate the bacterium from the vagina. However, if antibiotics are given at 38 or 39 weeks' gestation, the organism may be removed but return again before birth. The only way of reducing infection, therefore, is to give antibiotics to the mother during the birth process, though this is not accepted standard obstetric practice. Nor is it accepted practice to undertake vaginal swabs in all pregnant women to determine the presence or otherwise of Group B *Streptococcus*. The possibility of such an infection is always the first thought, therefore, in babies who clinically seem infected.

Diagnosis

The fetal lungs are filled with fluid in the womb. This fluid is removed during birth, partly by being squeezed out during passage through the birth canal and also by being drained away internally. If this fluid is not entirely removed, the baby has some breathing difficulty and may begin to grunt during expiration as a way of improving oxygen and carbon dioxide exchange. This grunting is more frequent in babies born by caesarean section, as they do not undergo the squeezing of a vaginal birth. The grunting normally resolves in a few hours. Group B *Streptococcus* causing pneumonia in the unborn baby will also cause grunting respiration after birth.

Treatment

Most baby units will have a policy, therefore, for starting broad spectrum antibiotics in babies if there has been a history of prolonged rupture of membranes, normally taken as greater than 24 hours, or if the baby develops grunting respiration. There is no universally accepted combination of antibiotics, but the combinations give broad cover against many bacteria, including Group B *Streptococcus*. Prompt administration of antibiotics after birth thus reduces the severity of any infection. Unfortunately some babies are heavily infected in the hours before birth and, despite timely antibiotics and full intensive care, do not survive or survive with major damage, often neurological. Hospital units should have clear antibiotic policies concerning which, and in what circumstances, antibiotics should be commenced.

Case study: delayed antibiotics causing death in a newborn baby

Clare was Lindsay's second baby. The pregnancy was planned; Lindsay had attended for antenatal care and was booked for delivery at the local maternity unit, which happened to have full intensive care baby facilities. All went well and Lindsay's waters broke on the expected day of delivery. She presented to hospital and delivered Clare some 20 hours later. Mother and daughter went to the postnatal ward. Around two hours of life, Clare was noticed to be grunting and had an apnoeic episode (stopped breathing for a few seconds). She was seen by a junior doctor who felt that she should be admitted to the baby unit for observation. This was duly done, and Clare was reviewed four hours later by a more senior paediatrician as the nursing staff were anxious about her clinical deterioration. Full intensive care was commenced, intravenous antibiotics administered and more senior help summoned. Despite several hours of exemplary intensive care, Clare died, aged 18 hours.

The claimants argued that there were sufficient clinical grounds for antibiotics to have been administered immediately Clare had been admitted to the unit. Had the antibiotics been thus administered, instead of after a delay of four hours, Clare would have survived.

The defendants admitted liability in that their neonatal policy clearly stated that antibiotics should be given to babies who developed grunting respiration, but argued causation, stating that as Clare had died so quickly she must have had overwhelming sepsis in the womb and therefore the omission of antibiotics for four hours made no difference to outcome.

Expert witnesses came to opposing views as to the importance of those few hours. One argued that the prenatal overwhelming sepsis would not have been affected by earlier antibiotics. The other felt that as Clare had been entirely well clinically at birth, showed no deterioration until two hours of age, and was relatively well until six hours of life, postnatal evolution of the infection was important, so the omission of antibiotics for four hours significantly compromised Clare's chances of survival. The experts agreed to meet and concluded that the omission of antibiotics was negligent. They agreed that it was not possible, either from this specific case or from medical literature, to place a sensible estimate of Clare's chances of survival had antibiotics been given on admission to the unit, but accepted that her chances of survival had been compromised by the delay.

The Trust agreed to cover funeral expenses as a goodwill gesture, but did not accept liability.

RETINOPATHY OF PREMATURITY

Retinopathy of prematurity (ROP), or retrolental fibroplasia, as it was previously known, is a potential cause of visual impairment and blindness in premature infants. The blood vessels in the retina grow out from the point where both the nerve to the eye (optic nerve) and the blood supply enter the eyeball. This point, the optic disc, is placed eccentrically closer to the nose than to the side of the head, the temple. The blood vessels grow outwards during development and reach the edge of the retina on the nasal side sooner than on the temporal side. Once the blood vessels reach the border of the retina, no further growth is necessary and they are not vulnerable to the factors causing ROP. Thus the blood vessels heading towards the temporal side of the retina are vulnerable to those factors for longer than those heading towards the nasal side. The vasculature of the retina is complete by 32–34 weeks' gestation; after this ROP is no longer a problem.

Mechanism of ROP

It has been recognised for many years that high oxygen levels in the blood cause ROP. This led to constant monitoring of the amount of oxygen being delivered to babies. However, a belief arose in the late 1970s and early 1980s that as long as the concentration of oxygen the baby was breathing did not exceed 40%, there was no danger of ROP. This was, and is, an erroneous belief, because what is important is the concentration of oxygen in the blood being delivered to the retinal blood vessels, not the concentration being delivered to the baby's lungs.

Prevention of ROP

This oxygen concentration in the blood depends on the percentage of oxygen being breathed and the health of the baby's lungs. Thus monitoring of blood oxygen levels became mandatory. This occurred in several ways. In intermittent blood gas analysis, arterial blood was taken from the baby either by an indwelling catheter in the aorta fed through the umbilical cord, or from puncture of a peripheral artery, frequently the radial artery in the wrist. The sample would be analysed for the content of oxygen, carbon dioxide and acid. These analyses would be undertaken every four hours or so. Attempts were made to monitor oxygen levels constantly via an electrode in the aorta. These electrodes were highly unreliable and frequently correlated poorly with blood gas analysis. The next stage of constant monitoring was by transcutaneous oxygen analysis. An electrode was applied closely to the baby's skin and the skin heated to around 40°C by a heating coil in the electrode. This dilated the capillaries in the underlying skin, so allowing more blood flow through the capillaries and making blood oxygen levels reasonably similar to arterial. The electrode sensed oxygen diffusing through the skin. This method was quite successful. Once calibrated, many electrodes were stable, the only problem being the necessity to change the site of the electrodes every four hours to prevent burning of the skin. Nowadays the most commonly used constant measure is oxygen saturation – this measures the amount of haemoglobin which has oxygen attached compared to that free of oxygen. In normal healthy adults this ranges from 98–100%. It is impossible to know whether at 100% saturation the oxygen content of the blood is normal, at approximately 12 kPa (100 mmg), or whether it is far higher. Thus in premature babies at risk of ROP, oxygen saturation is kept at less than or equal to 94–96%. At these levels there is reasonable security that blood oxygen levels are not high enough to cause ROP.

Likelihood of occurrence of ROP

Despite these precautions ROP still does occur, as oxygen concentration is not the only trigger for developing ROP, but we do not know all the factors that are important. The only undisputed requirement is prematurity, some other factors implicated being excess light and vitamin deficiency.

Stages and management of ROP

There are four stages of ROP. Stages 1 and 2 require follow-up, but resolve spontaneously. Stages 3 and 4 normally need operative intervention to prevent progression to retinal detachment and visual impairment. Intervention is either by laser therapy through the pupil, or cryotherapy (freezing small parts of the retina from the back of the eyeball). All babies born before 32 weeks are at risk of ROP, but different paediatric ophthalmologists have different criteria for examining premature babies for ROP. In my own unit all babies of 32 weeks' gestation and under are examined, with their pupils chemically dilated, from six weeks of age. The ophthalmologist determines the follow-up plan. This two-pronged approach of constantly monitoring oxygen saturation and ophthalmic examination of at-risk babies has dramatically reduced the incidence of severe visual loss from ROP.

Case study: screening for ROP, acceptable standards in earlier times

Hardeep was the first successful pregnancy after many attempts and early miscarriages. However, Hardeep's mother went into premature labour in 1988 at 26 weeks' gestation. She was transferred to a maternity unit with neonatal intensive care facilities. Hardeep was immediately transferred to the baby unit and ventilated from birth. He had considerable problems with his lungs, requiring high inspired oxygen concentration to keep blood oxygen levels at acceptable values. As his lungs improved the inspired oxygen concentration was not reduced in keeping with the clinical improvement, and very high blood oxygen levels were recorded on several occasions. Eventually Hardeep made a good recovery and was discharged home. At follow-up in Outpatients, his parents expressed concern about his sight, as he did not appear to be looking at them and would not respond to a bright light such as a torch. The paediatrician agreed and referred Hardeep to a paediatric ophthalmologist, who diagnosed retinal detachment secondary to ROP and indicated that Hardeep was blind. Over the years it became obvious that

Hardeep was developing entirely normally given the restrictions caused by his blindness.

Hardeep's parents sought legal advice in 1995, arguing that it was known that high oxygen levels were a cause of ROP. Hardeep had had frequent documented high blood oxygen levels and so should have been reviewed by a paediatric ophthalmologist whilst still an in-patient. Developing ROP would have been diagnosed, allowing early operative intervention with consequent preservation of some vision.

The paediatric expert witness agreed that there were high levels of blood oxygen recorded in Hardeep's notes and that these, despite other potential causes, on the balance of probabilities caused Hardeep's ROP. However, the overall standard of care Hardeep had received was excellent and in 1988 intermittent sampling of blood gases was acceptable practice.

The ophthalmic expert again agreed that the ROP was probably secondary to the high blood oxygen levels, but routine ophthalmic screening for ROP was not widely available in 1988 and normal practice was to refer high-risk babies to the ophthalmologist after discharge from the baby unit. Hardeep's unit had, therefore, acted in a way that was entirely acceptable in 1988. The case did not proceed. Clearly this standard of care could not be defended for today's babies, but cases must be judged on the standards prevailing at that time, not retrospectively by the standards present at the time of litigation.

CHAPTER 6

CONGENITAL DYSPLASIA OF THE HIPS

Congenital dysplasia of the hips (CDH) used to be known as congenital dislocation of the hips. However, it has become clear that not all problems with the hips are recognisable, or even present, at birth and dislocation can occur over the first few months of life.

THE HIP JOINT

The hip joint is a ball-and-socket joint. The top of the femur (the long bone in the upper leg) ends in a ball which fits into a socket covering some 60% or so of the ball. This makes the joint very stable. The socket, or acetabulum, is partially formed by the pressure exerted on the pelvis via the femur. This occurs partly from the pressure exerted by the muscles between the pelvis, backbone and femur, but more so by the pressure transmitted up the femur from the baby's weight, for example, in a baby walker, baby bouncer or when crawling. If the hip is, or becomes, dislocated the acetabulum does not develop, remains shallow and cannot accept the ball, or head, of the femur securely without operation.

SCREENING FOR CDH

CDH is tested for shortly after birth, when all babies are examined by junior doctors. Two tests are undertaken: Ortolani and Barlow. Ortolani's test consists of abduction of the hips (pushing the hips apart), and Barlow's test consists of attempting to sublux (partially dislocate) the hip joint by pushing the upper leg backwards when the baby is lying on its back, to determine whether there is any instability. These two tests try to screen for actual and partial dislocation, and they should be undertaken in all babies, even in those discharged a few hours after birth. The checks must also be repeated at the six-week baby examination. Unfortunately, there is no consensus amongst paediatricians or paediatric orthopaedic surgeons as to the best way of examining hips. Some units will examine all babies clinically and also by ultrasound of the hip, others will ultrasound all babies, yet others will examine all babies clinically and ultrasound only those babies in whom the clinical examination is abnormal, as well as those at high risk.

HIGH-RISK CATEGORIES FOR CDH

It is recognised that there are high-risk groups for CDH. These are those babies in whom there is a family history of CDH, or those babies born in the breech position. These babies should be examined carefully. There seems to be reasonable agreement between paediatricians and paediatric orthopaedic surgeons that high-risk babies should, as a minimum, have an ultrasound of the hips.

EARLY TREATMENT FOR CDH

If abnormalities are found, that is, dislocation or subluxation (not dislocated, but able to be partially dislocated), then intervention in the form of a harness is needed. Again, there is no consensus as to which is the best particular type of harness, but there is universal agreement that active intervention in the first few weeks of life is mandatory. Such intervention normally is successful and obviates the need for later surgical procedures.

LATE PRESENTATION OF CDH

Unfortunately, despite the various screening procedures a few infants present later with dislocated hips, normally when they are beginning to walk, around the age of one year (range nine months to 18 months) when the parents notice the asymmetry of the legs, one being shorter than the other. By this time the acetabulum is shallow and covered by tissue, so the hip joint is unstable unless the child undergoes an operation.

LATE TREATMENT FOR CDH

Intervention in late presenting dislocated hip requires major surgical procedures over several months. Initially an acetabulum is formed in the pelvis and the head of the femur placed within the new socket. However, the only way the joint can be stabilised is by forcing the leg into an entirely abnormal position. The hip joint is then stabilised by a fixed solid plaster-of-Paris splint: a spica. This covers the entire pelvis, so fixing the abnormal hip by being stabilised by the normal hip. The child is effectively in plaster from the waist downwards for several months. This not surprisingly causes immense problems with hygiene. When there has been bony healing of the pelvis, the second stage of correction is derotational oseotomy. This means the femur is surgically broken, the leg is rotated into its normal position and fixed with internal metal fixings, and another lower body spica is applied for several months. At the end of these procedures the child is considerably scarred, there can still be a difference in leg length, and over the years the head of the femur can dissolve (necrosis), which shortens the leg even further. There is likely to be premature arthritis in that joint also.

Missing a CDH thus potentially has a major effect on a young child's life and also thereafter, during childhood and adult life. The many months of hospital visits also considerably disrupt family life. Not surprisingly, litigation springs to mind in such circumstances. Despite screening tests, it has been repeatedly demonstrated that a few children who were passed as entirely normal in the first few weeks of life develop CDH later. Therefore, the development of CDH does not automatically imply negligence. Indeed, if it is clearly documented that the relevant checks were undertaken and, if indicated in high-risk babies, more detailed examination undertaken, negligence has not occurred. Negligence can only be contemplated if either the hips were not checked in hospital or during community baby checks, or that ultrasound or special vigilance was not undertaken in the two high-risk groups.

Case study: failure of hip check causing late diagnosis of CDH

Sophie presented at 14 months of age with a limping gait. Examination revealed a relatively shorter right leg, and x-ray confirmed CDH, which was corrected by open operative reduction. The claimants argued that the CDH must have been present at birth and was negligently missed by the examining paediatricians. Reference to the notes revealed that the baby examination had been diligently undertaken and the pre-printed notes completed, apart from any comment about hip examination. Her mother had not taken Sophie to the six-week check as she herself had been unwell, so the next contact with the medical profession was at eight months.

The defence argued that Sophie's mother was to blame for not having taken her to the six-week check and that, on the balance of probabilities, the hip check had been undertaken as the rest of the examination had been so thorough. The claimants maintained that the defence could not prove that Sophie did not have CDH at birth, which should have been found, and that absence of comment concerning the hip examination equated to absence of hip examination. Expert advice was that the case was indefensible because of the absence of documentation of the hip check. Liability was admitted and the case settled out of court.

Case study: failure of six-week hip check causing late diagnosis of CDH

Rachel similarly presented with a limping gait at 12 months. She also underwent open reduction for CDH. It was argued that the problem should have been discovered at birth. The hospital notes revealed that Rachel had a clicking right hip and she was referred to a consultant paediatrician's clinic, aged four weeks. It was clearly documented that she was not in a high-risk category and that both Ortolani and Barlow tests had been performed and both were negative. No negligence was proven. However, it was discovered that a repeat hip screen had been omitted at the six-week baby clinic. The claimants argued successfully that negligence at the six-week check allowed the late presentation of CDH. Again the matter was settled out of court.

It is defensible to miss a CDH as long as the hip check is carried out and unequivocally recorded. What is not acceptable is either omitting the hip check, even though the hips may have been examined recently, or omitting to record that examination was undertaken.

CHAPTER 7

PAEDIATRIC CARE IN THE NHS

INTRODUCTION

Medical care in the National Health Service (NHS) is traditionally divided into primary, secondary, and tertiary care. Primary care refers to the medical care afforded in general practice. Secondary care is hospital-based care, that is, when the patient is referred from their own general practitioner (GP) to a hospital consultant. Tertiary care refers to hospital-based care when the patient is referred from one hospital consultant to another.

Secondary care, broadly speaking, occurs in district general hospitals, although some tertiary hospitals will also act as the district general hospital for that particular area.

Tertiary care occurs predominantly in teaching hospitals, although there may be tertiary services in some local district general hospitals. The term 'teaching hospital' used here refers to the main hospital attached to the medical school of a university. There are now many hospitals affiliated to university medical schools, which have been given teaching hospital status because of the increasing number of medical students that are being trained at present. The original teaching hospital, though, is still recognisable and the tertiary services still tend to be concentrated there as many of these services are interdependent.

PRIMARY CARE

Strictly speaking, all patients belong to their GP, who still carries ultimate responsibility for the total care of his patients. The GP refers patients for a specialist opinion concerning certain aspects of the medical care and the hospital consultant forwards that opinion. Formerly the hospital consultant would see and examine the patient and then write back to the GP with his opinion. Little communication occurred between the hospital consultant and patient, as it was felt that the GP had asked for an opinion and therefore that opinion should be rendered to the GP, not to the patient! This practice has now changed and the patient, rightly, expects a full discussion with the consultant following the consultation. However, the GP still retains overall care for that patient.

PRIMARY/SECONDARY SHARED CARE

Shared care of such patients, therefore, exists *de facto*. Although the hospital specialist may diagnose the illness and prescribe treatment, it is the GP who still ministers to the patient on a day to day basis, even though the GP may have either limited or even no experience of the particular illness. Clear and precise communication from the hospital consultant to the GP is, therefore, mandatory. It is completely unacceptable to expect the GP to have the same degree of knowledge about a particular diagnosis as a specialist hospital consultant. Consequently, medico-legally a GP's knowledge and practice must be judged by the standards of his peers, that is other GPs, not judged against the standard of hospital consultants.

Examples of such shared care would be GP clinics in diabetes or in asthma. Some GPs do not wish to participate actively in the care of patients with diabetes; others will run regular diabetes clinics at the surgery but share care with the local hospital diabetes clinic; yet other GPs may wish to take on the entire care of uncomplicated diabetes. A similar scenario may exist with asthma. However, there are few GPs who would undertake the care of children with diabetes on a regular basis, as the number of children with diabetes in a particular GP practice is very small, hence the GP will have relatively little experience in looking after such children. This may be contrasted with asthma. Many children develop asthma, indeed the incidence of asthma in the school-age population is increasing. It is, therefore, perfectly acceptable for GPs to take on the care of children with asthma as it is so common and GPs are well experienced in its care. However, having made the decision to take on the care of specific patients, be they adults or children, with a particular disease then it is expected that the GP would have equal knowledge of that disease to that of a hospital-based consultant. In this instance, therefore, any medico-legal discussions would compare the GP with the specialist hospital consultant and not with the GP's own peers.

SECONDARY CARE

There are as yet few guidelines as to what illnesses may be looked after in general practice and which need to be referred to hospital. Clearly there are instances when the GP cannot undertake treatment, such as major surgery, but the dividing line between which illnesses and diseases can be managed in general practice care and which need hospital care is blurred indeed. It therefore becomes a value judgment as to whether any particular patient should have been referred onwards from the GP or not.

The GP sees the vast majority of patients and refers on to hospital only a small percentage of his caseload. Hospital consultants undertaking secondary care often have a degree of specialisation but frequently have to undertake general medical care of their patients. This is particularly true in paediatric medicine. There is not the same degree of specialisation in paediatric medicine that exists in adult medicine, and this relates entirely to the relatively small numbers of children attending hospital as opposed to adults. In the small district general hospitals, therefore, there may only be four or five paediatricians, all of whom would look after general paediatric care, although they may have a particular specialty interest, for example, asthma, diabetes or kidney disease. Even in larger secondary units, which may have 10–15 consultants, those consultants would still be predominantly general paediatricians, although they are much more likely to have a specialist interest also.

These consultants would decide whether to continue following up the children referred to them by the GP, to refer them back to the GP, or to refer them onwards to the tertiary centre where the hospital-based consultants are predominantly specialist consultants, rather than being general paediatricians. Such tertiary services are frequently organised along the lines of organs, such as cardiologists (heart specialists), nephrologists (kidney specialists), or gastroenterologists (gut specialists).

TERTIARY CARE

Tertiary services specially for children are considerably limited. There is therefore a high degree of filtering of patients by the secondary care hospital consultants so that very few children are referred on to the paediatric specialists. Ideally, the tertiary specialist should refer a patient back to the secondary hospital consultant or GP when the particular expertise possessed by the tertiary consultant is no longer necessary for that particular patient. These two systems, filtering before referral and referring back as soon as possible, should allow tertiary services to be afforded to those children who truly need such specialist care.

SECONDARY/TERTIARY SHARED CARE

This again leads to the concept of shared care either between the tertiary and secondary consultants or between the tertiary consultant and the GP. Again, clear communication between the tertiary consultant and the other professionals is mandatory.

Some of these children have to travel many hours for a relatively short outpatient consultation in the tertiary centre. A more efficient system, therefore, is for these children to be seen at their local hospital, with only intermittent consultations at the tertiary hospital. Some children may elect to bypass their local hospital and only attend the specialist centre. This system is acceptable until a crisis intervenes. Should such a child become suddenly and critically ill, then they are in the first instance admitted to their local hospital for stabilisation. If the child is unknown at the local hospital and the illness is sufficiently complex for the local paediatricians not to be well versed in its treatment and complications, this can lead to compromised medical care for the child. Conversely, if such children are well known and have free access to the local hospital then their care, both routine and emergency, can be foreseen and planned.

WARD PASSPORT

One way to improve communication between centres is for the family to carry a 'passport'. This is a document that details the child's illness, symptoms and potential complications. These complications then have treatment regimens associated with them. Thus the family can be reassured that wherever problems arise appropriate care can be given to the child in a timely fashion, regardless of the local knowledge or expertise with respect to that illness.

A passport is also used to allow children to gain immediate access to the paediatric unit in their local or specialist hospital, so time is not lost waiting for the GP or explaining the problem time and again in the Accident and Emergency department. Although this approach seems common sense, it is by no means universal.

These two groups of consultants must therefore be judged by their peers. Secondary hospital consultants will have a broader based knowledge of paediatrics, whilst the specialist consultants will have a narrow width of knowledge but considerable depth. However, secondary consultants must recognise their own limitations when dealing with complex children or illnesses. It is perfectly acceptable for a secondary paediatrician not to have detailed knowledge of a particular condition, but it is not acceptable for such a paediatrician to 'have a go' in the absence of detailed knowledge. There must either be rapid referral on to the specialist centre or, if treatment is to be effected at the local hospital, this must be with communication between the secondary and tertiary hospital consultants or, as a minimum, between experienced junior doctors.

Case study: failure of diagnosis and failure of communication in an unfamiliar child with a complicated illness

Darryl was born with a complex heart problem. This necessitated several operations on his heart in the major children's heart unit that was 60 miles away from his home. Eventually it was considered that his heart condition was stable following the construction of a conduit outside his heart, the result of the so called Fontan's procedure. He was seen in Outpatients every six months at the central heart unit and did not attend his local district general hospital. Initially the cardiologist sent letters both to Darryl's GP and to the local hospital consultant. However, there was a change of cardiologist and no further letters were sent to the local hospital consultant.

When Darryl was 10 years old he developed gastroenteritis with copious vomiting and diarrhoea. His mother called the GP, who saw Darryl at home and noted that he had a very irregular heart rate. The GP checked his own records and noted that each time Darryl had been to Outpatients the cardiologist had noted that Darryl's pulse was regular. The GP himself contacted the medical staff at the heart unit, who advised the GP to send Darryl to the local hospital for an ECG (a heart tracing) in case an abnormal heartbeat had developed. Darryl was seen by the paediatric registrar who undertook the ECG, which he felt was normal, and discharged Darryl home with advice to return if he worsened.

Darryl's gastroenteritis did not improve, so his mother asked for another GP visit. This second GP called at the home where he found that Darryl was dehydrated. He recommended clear fluids and arranged to return that afternoon. At this visit he noted that Darryl was worse, so referred him up to the local hospital again. Examination revealed that Darryl was still dehydrated and that he had a very irregular heartbeat. The cardiac centre was contacted and they advised cardioversion (electrical shock to put the heart back to a normal rhythm) followed by immediate transfer to the cardiac centre. The local paediatrician did not feel experienced enough to undertake cardioversion, so arranged urgent transfer. However, just before Darryl was moved to the ambulance he suffered a cardiac arrest and could not be resuscitated. Post mortem showed a blood clot that had obstructed the artery to the lungs.

The claimants argued that Darryl should have been properly assessed and either kept in the local hospital or referred to the cardiac centre the first time that he was referred by the GP. If that had happened Darryl's condition could have been monitored, he would not have become dehydrated, and the fatal blood clot would not have formed.

The defendants claimed that the paediatric registrar who undertook the ECG had properly assessed Darryl and that Darryl became dehydrated because his mother had failed to heed medical advice to keep him drinking or to return to the hospital if he got worse.

Review of the first ECG demonstrated that Darryl was suffering from atrial fibrillation (rapid ineffective contraction of the collecting chambers of the heart) which the paediatric registrar had failed to diagnose, this despite the letter from the GP which clearly stated that Darryl's heart rate was irregular and that the cardiac unit had recommended an ECG specifically to rule out atrial fibrillation. The combination of Darryl's underlying complex heart problem and atrial fibrillation produced a situation where clot formation in the heart was significantly increased. The correct method of treating Darryl, therefore, would have been to have diagnosed atrial fibrillation on the first ECG and commenced him on anticoagulants. This would have reduced the chances of clot formation in the heart.

The defendants admitted that atrial fibrillation had been misdiagnosed on the first ECG, but argued that this was a very rare complication of a complicated heart defect. It was not unreasonable, therefore, that the paediatric registrar and consultant were unaware either of this complication or of the need for anticoagulants if atrial fibrillation supervened.

The claimants accepted that it was reasonable that neither doctor was aware of this unusual complication and its subsequent treatment. However, if they were not familiar with the complications of complex heart lesions and the effect of their corrective operations then there should have been immediate consultation with the heart centre, as indeed the GP had done.

The judge found for the claimants, accepting the argument that a general paediatrician faced with an unknown patient with a complex problem did not have to know the exquisite details of that problem but should recognise his own limitations and seek assistance from the specialist cardiologists. The judge held that the defendants had been negligent in not diagnosing atrial fibrillation. He also held that the causative link had been established in that the omission of anticoagulants increased the likelihood of clot formation in the heart.

RARE DISEASES

This situation is further exacerbated in those children who have extremely rare illnesses which may allow the child to lead a normal life for most of the time but which include a catastrophic reaction to minor illnesses. Rapid resuscitation and stabilisation is necessary, but also the use of specific drugs or fluids may be needed to improve the chances of the child surviving such a catastrophic deterioration.

The rarity of these diseases may be such that only one or two hospitals have sufficiently specialist departments to diagnose and institute treatment. It is also important that such rare children are treated only in a very few hospitals, so that expertise may be increased as the natural progress of these illnesses is followed and better understood. However, if children are gathered from across the UK, but still constitute a very small number, then local hospitals will have very little experience of the disease either in its quiescent or catastrophic state. Again, clear communication is mandatory between the centre and the local hospitals. This must include not only letters detailing routine progress of the child but also guidelines for emergency treatment at the local hospital should they present in the local Accident and Emergency department. It is also sensible for the family to have a copy of the emergency treatment guidelines so that appropriate care can be afforded the child wherever they present. In this complex situation it would be inappropriate for a GP to refer such a child to the specialist hospital. If the child is very sick, he must be stabilised in the local hospital first before transfer to the specialist hospital, if that is indeed necessary.

LOCAL OR SPECIALIST CARE?

There is always a tension between wishing to provide as much service to the local paediatric population in the local hospital and recognising that certain children need the expertise that can only be found in large paediatric departments, be they specialist departments in teaching hospitals or be they departments in large district general hospitals. The increasing complexity of operative and diagnostic possibilities means that children who previously would have died are being kept alive, sometimes with a considerable life expectancy.

Paediatric practice has evolved, therefore, into a multi-layered service with increasing specialist knowledge and skill at each level. Thus the child referred to hospital by the GP may find himself cared for by that particular hospital consultant, or that consultant may refer on to one of his colleagues in the same hospital who has greater expertise in that particular area. The general paediatrician with a special interest may continue to care for this child, or refer on to a specialist who deals only with children with that particular disease. That specialist paediatrician may continue with the care of the child or may refer on to another more specialised unit at a different specialist hospital. The change in some of these layers implies increasing distance from the child's home, with concomitant increasing difficulty in communication between specialist and local hospital.

The importance of communication has been stressed frequently in this chapter, as failure in communication can lead to negligent care of the child, who rightly deserves the best possible care regardless of his illness or disease and regardless of the care environment into which the child is admitted.

CHAPTER 8

GENERAL PAEDIATRIC CARE

INTRODUCTION

The practice of general paediatric medical care involves several distinct but interrelated steps, regardless of whether the child presents as an emergency to the Accident and Emergency department or whether he is referred up routinely to general Paediatric Outpatients. A history is elicited, during which the paediatrician attempts to define the problem or problems. At the end of such a history clues should have been gleaned which point the paediatrician in the direction of the correct diagnosis and this then influences the emphasis of the subsequent physical examination.

Medical students are taught to undertake a full examination of every patient; the rationale of this is that their history-taking may not be particularly sophisticated so that a full physical examination is necessary in order to reduce the chances of missing physical signs that the child may have developed. With increasing expertise, history-taking becomes more skilled and so the physical examination is usually concentrated on the particular area of the child that seems most likely to hold further clues to the underlying illness as elicited earlier by the history.

Extra evidence may be necessary in the form of investigations, such as blood tests or other more sophisticated investigations. Once the diagnosis has been elucidated a decision is made as to whether treatment is necessary or not. Active treatment may be either to continue along the medical model, or a decision may be required for further referral, for example, to paediatric surgery. Mistakes can therefore be made during any part of this interrelated chain of events, leading to a misdiagnosis. Treatment options may suffer a similarly mistaken choice. Appropriate treatment may mistakenly be withheld, inappropriate treatment given, or appropriate treatment ordered and mistakes made in administration thereof.

INADEQUATE HISTORY

The accuracy of a detailed history is of considerable importance. It is the start of a train of events that may culminate in a child receiving treatment. A quickly taken or incorrectly interpreted history can influence the subsequent examination and investigations, with a result that an erroneous diagnosis is made and erroneous treatment suggested.

The emphasis of the history will alter depending on the age of the child. For example, obstetric and birth history are of considerable importance in a young child who presents with delayed development. Antenatal history is of less importance in an adolescent presenting with diabetes mellitus. Family history is universally important in that some diseases run in families, such as kidney problems. Other diseases may start with that particular generation but several siblings or near relatives may have the same problem. Failure to elucidate such familial tendencies reduces the chance of an accurate diagnosis.

Case study: inadequate history leading to avoidable early death

Shahid and Indira had three children, and Indira was expecting her fourth child. Their second child, Mohammed, was on regular tablets. Shahid and Indira attended the antenatal clinic regularly once they realised that Indira was pregnant. Shahid gave the answers to the obstetrician's questions, as Indira did not speak English. The obstetrician noted in the family history that one son had 'a blood problem'.

The pregnancy continued uneventfully and Indira was delivered of a baby boy, Habib. The paediatric SHO reviewed the obstetric notes and noted the comments about the family history, but merely congratulated Shahid and Indira on their new son. The SHO noted that Habib's testicles were not present, took some blood tests, discharged Habib and arranged for an outpatient appointment after Christmas, some six weeks away.

At 12 days of age, Habib was rushed into the Accident and Emergency department in a collapsed state, having been vomiting for two days. Despite intensive resuscitation he sadly died. The consultant paediatrician who had been called for the resuscitation recognised the family as he had been looking after the elder child for congenital adrenal hyperplasia.

The blood investigations taken from Habib shortly after birth indicated that he was in fact a girl with congenital adrenal hyperplasia and that she had died because she had not received the appropriate treatment.

The claimants claimed that the family history should have been known and that, even if the family was not entirely clear of the diagnosis, a comment such as 'a blood disorder' should have prompted a more detailed examination of the family history and family notes.

The Trust admitted liability.

Case study: misinterpretation of bruising in a young baby

Brian was born at full term following an uncomplicated pregnancy. He was the first child of Mary, a single parent, but supported by her partner, Steve. At the age of four weeks Mary brought Brian to the Accident and Emergency department because she was worried that Brian had suddenly developed bruises on his legs for no obvious reason.

The paediatric SHO in her history noted that Brian was breast-fed and, although he had been given vitamin K at birth, wondered whether he had a blood clotting disorder caused by a deficiency of vitamin K. Clotting studies were normal, so Brian was discharged home.

Two weeks later the ambulance service received an emergency call and Brian was found fitting by the paramedics. His seizures were controlled in the Accident and Emergency department. A CT scan of his head revealed extensive bleeding between the brain and the inner surface of the skull. The blood was evacuated but over the subsequent months it became clear that Brian had suffered a major insult to the brain and developed severe learning difficulties.

His father was charged and convicted of non-accidental injury. The initial bruises at the age of four weeks were finger marks where his father had grasped Brian with excess force. The cause of the bleeding around the brain was due to his father shaking him violently.

The initial thought by the paediatric SHO of clotting disorder was entirely appropriate, even in a baby who was breast-fed and given vitamin K at birth. However, once the clotting studies had been found to be normal then an alternative cause for the bruising must be sought in an infant not yet old enough to bruise itself. Bruising in young babies must always raise the possibility of non-accidental injury, even if this proves not to be the eventual diagnosis.

DRUG THERAPY

Modern medical therapy relies heavily on drug treatment. There are now numerous drugs available within paediatric practice and numerous options are frequently available to treat the same type of illness.

Drug therapy is very young in the history of medicine and the regulations required for introducing a new drug onto the market have changed significantly in the last 60 years. Drugs that have been available for many years were subjected to considerably less scientific rigour before introduction than is applied now. Presently the development of new drugs is subjected to intense scrutiny and highly controlled therapeutic trials before the drug is licensed for general release.

There are considerable ethical concerns about subjecting children to experimental drugs, not least because the children themselves are unable to give consent for their bodies to be used experimentally. This has led, therefore, to drug trials been undertaken in adults and then the drug dosage being scaled down for children, even though it is recognised that children's bodies react differently to those of adults to the same drug. Thus a large percentage of drugs which are used in children are prescribed 'off licence', that is, the drug has never been experimentally tried in children and therefore does not have a licence for use in children. However, without these drugs there would be unnecessary childhood morbidity and mortality.

Paediatric drug therapy is therefore complicated by having to calculate differing drug regimens for the same drug depending on the child's weight and age. This is additional to the complexity of the number of available drugs. Drug errors are therefore potentially easy to make. In an attempt to reduce the chances of such drug errors hospitals have introduced several safety measures.

Drug administration

The drug and dosage are prescribed by the paediatrician and these are then checked and signed off by the hospital pharmacist. During the ward drug round, two qualified nurses are present to recalculate the dosage of the drug. Each nurse checks the calculation of the other nurse, then checks the drug itself and, in the case of a liquid drug, checks the volume. The drug and the drug chart are then taken to the child's bedside, the drug checked against the drug chart, the drug chart checked against the child's identification band around its wrist, and only then is the drug administered to the child. There are therefore several checks between the initial prescription and the administration of the drug to minimise any chance of drug errors. How, then, can drug errors occur?

The vast majority, but not all, drug errors occur when one of these checks has not been followed or has broken down.

Wrong drug

This is potentially a more difficult problem to guard against. As mentioned above, there are often several alternative drugs for the same illness and there are many drugs with similar sounding names that may be used for completely different illnesses.

The hospital pharmacist does not usually know the diagnosis of the child. The main role of the hospital pharmacist is to check whether a drug is appropriate generally for children and that the dosage of the drug prescribed is correct. If, therefore, the paediatrician has prescribed the right dose of the wrong drug then it is possible that the pharmacist will sign off the hospital script as correct.

The nurses, however, will know the diagnosis of the child and should be able to guard against an inappropriate drug being used for the actual diagnosis of that particular child. However, one of the hospital checks has been breached, that is, that of the pharmacist. It is not difficult to imagine that nurses, who may be under considerable pressure, can check the calculation and dosage of the drug, find them to be correct and administer the correct dose of the wrong drug.

The pressures on nurses in the present NHS, which has removed large numbers of qualified nurses from wards, are such that there are frequent and often conflicting demands on their time. It is not unusual, therefore, for one of the nurses on the drug round to be called away for a few minutes to attend a sick child or to respond to a parental inquiry. It is at these times that drug errors may occur.

Wrong dose

The wrong dose of a drug can either be perpetrated by the wrong dose being prescribed initially by the paediatrician, or by miscalculation of the amount of the drug by the nurses.

The paediatric prescription is the first link in the chain. All drugs and doses are subjected to scrutiny by the hospital pharmacist and by the nurses and so, although it is possible for junior doctors, who may have had limited experience of paediatrics, to prescribe the wrong dose, this error should be corrected either by the pharmacist or by the nurses.

All intravenous drugs and many oral drugs in paediatric practice are in liquid form, and there are therefore two calculations for the administering nurses to undertake. One is to check the accuracy of the prescribed dosage, and the second is to dilute the prescribed dosage to the appropriate volume either for intravenous or for oral use. Not only are many drugs not licensed for paediatric practice, but many of the intravenous formulations are designed for adult usage, and so are in a highly concentrated form with respect to paediatric practice. Complex calculations are therefore required.

Again, two nurses are responsible for the calculation of the appropriate drug volume. Each nurse will calculate the volume independently and then compare their results. If there is discrepancy the calculations will be re-checked and re-checked until there is agreement. To add further to the complexity, some drugs or additives come in vials containing different concentrations of the same drug, requiring therefore very different dilution factors. It is not difficult to see that in this therapeutic area, with so many variables, errors are possible.

INTRAVENOUS FLUIDS

Wrong fluid

The daily fluid requirements alter dramatically depending on the size and age of the child. The feeling of thirst controls normal intake. There are also some controls to absorption of fluid, even if there is excess fluid ingestion. The fluid has to be transported across the lining of the stomach or of the guts, which can modify fluid absorption. However, if fluids are given directly into the veins there can be no such controls.

A new-born baby requires a very high volume of fluid relative to its size, 150 mls/kg/day, whereas a sizeable teenager may require only 30 mls/kg/day. Also babies and young children need frequent feeds and do not tolerate starvation well. There must, therefore, be careful attention to both the amount and type of fluid given to young children intravenously, which includes the amount of salt and the amount of sugar the child receives.

The typical fluid received intravenously by adults is salt water (normal saline); that given to children contains much less salt but added sugar (dextrose saline). Normal saline alone given to children will give far too much salt and inadequate sugar.

Case study: wrong intravenous fluid leading to fits and learning difficulties

Rob, aged two and a half years, was admitted with a cough and high temperature. Examination suggested that he was suffering from pneumonia, which was confirmed on chest x-ray. He was treated with appropriate intravenous antibiotics. However, he developed a local complication of forming pus between his lungs and chest wall. Despite aggressive treatment, Rob had to undergo surgical exploration of his chest with removal of the pus and debris caused by the pneumonia.

The chest surgeons admitted him to the intensive care unit for care of his chest drain. He was rehydrated with intravenous fluids. The chest surgeons wrote up an appropriate volume of fluid, but prescribed normal saline. The following day he began to fit and an urgent paediatric review was requested. Investigation revealed that Rob had a very low blood sugar, and his fits resolved when he was given intravenous glucose. His fluids were changed to dextrose saline.

After discharge it became clear that Rob was suffering from mild developmental delay which had not been present before his operation. The claimants argued that Rob had been given the wrong intravenous fluids for his age and that had he been given dextrose saline instead of normal saline he would not have suffered fits nor mild developmental delay.

The hospital admitted liability.

FLUID BALANCE

The daily fluid requirements in children decrease considerably as measured per kg per day in the first few years of life. We all have an obligatory water loss in sweat, urine, faeces and from breathing. The smaller the child the more rapidly it can become dehydrated, if either water loss increases, for example, during vomiting and diarrhoea, or if their water intake decreases, for example, if they refuse to drink because they are so ill. Thus when sick young children come into hospital they are often quite dehydrated.

It is quite difficult to make an accurate objective assessment of the degree of dehydration, and therefore of the amount of fluid needed for replacement over and above the normal fluid required for maintenance. There must be very careful attention to the amount of fluid given to young children intravenously, as the consequences of fluid overload can include swelling of the brain and also water logging of the lungs, making gas exchange difficult.

Case study: over-zealous rehydration causing death by respiratory failure

Farzana, aged six, developed diarrhoea and vomiting. She was taken to her GP who prescribed Diorylate (a sugar and salt rehydration fluid) for 24 hours. She did not, however, improve and the GP recommended that she should be admitted to hospital. By this time she was quite dehydrated, she was drowsy and had a fast heart rate, indicative of a low blood volume.

It was decided to rehydrate Farzana intravenously. It was estimated that she had lost 10% of her body weight in fluid so her intravenous replacement volume was calculated as her normal daily allowance plus the 10% loss, to be given over 24 hours.

Eighteen hours later her blood pressure began to drop. This was interpreted as being because she was still dehydrated as she had continued to have diarrhoea and vomiting. She was given a dose of protein solution and the volume of intravenous fluids was increased. Her blood pressure did not improve and she was given another dose of protein solution. She then began to develop breathing difficulties and required ventilation. Despite ventilation it became impossible to effect adequate gas exchange and, following discussions with her parents, Farzana was allowed to die following discontinuation of intensive care.

Her parents could not understand why a child who had only had vomiting and diarrhoea should not recover, and so commissioned an independent medical opinion. Analysis of the fluid regimen demonstrated that Farzana had been given three times her maintenance fluid initially, secondary to miscalculation of her hourly fluid requirements. This had been compounded by the two protein solution doses and also by the subsequent further increase in her intravenous fluids. The drop in her blood pressure indicated that her heart was overloaded and was beginning to fail, and this was not recognised by the medical staff. The ventilation problems were caused by water logging of the lungs, which effectively meant that Farzana drowned. This again was not recognised by the medical staff, so no treatment to reverse the fluid overload had been instituted.

The hospital admitted full liability.

Extravasation of intravenous fluids

Intravenous fluids or intravenous drugs are administered via a soft silicone cannula that is introduced into the lumen of the vein. However soft the material used to make the cannula, there is almost an inevitability that eventually the cannula tip will erode through the vein, so that any fluid introduced via the cannula will be forced into the tissues surrounding the vein rather than into the blood stream itself. This is well recognised in paediatric practice, and so care is taken firstly to fix the cannula in such a way that it cannot move much, so reducing the chances of rupture through the vein wall. Secondly, the site of the cannula should be inspected hourly if there is a constant infusion, or the site inspected each time a dose of intravenous drug is given. Many of the pumps used to infuse intravenous fluids have a pressure monitor. Hourly reading of the pressure in the pump should give an indication that there is a problem, in that the pressure needed to infuse fluids into the vein is very low but into the tissues is very high.

The erosion of the vein wall by an intravenous cannula is in itself not negligent, it happens very frequently. However, inadequate observation allowing excess fluid to be pumped into the surrounding tissues is negligent.

The main cause of damage to the surrounding tissues is via a pressure effect. The fluid is continuously pumped into the tissues and, although there is a degree of elasticity in the tissues and skin, eventually the pressure in the area becomes so great that the blood supply to the tissues is cut off, causing damage and death to those tissues.

Certain drugs such as sodium bicarbonate, or electrolytes such as calcium, or fluids such as intravenous nutrition, worsen the pressure damage to the surrounding tissues by causing chemical burns which can destroy the tissue completely. Extreme care must be taken, therefore, when using such locally irritant drugs or chemicals if the vein used is peripheral, for example, on the back of the hand. It is safer to introduce a long soft catheter into the vein, the end of which lies in the large vessels nearer the heart. These soft catheters are less likely to erode through the vein wall and also the chemical irritant factor of the fluid is diluted in the large volume of blood passing by.

Once fluid or chemicals are in the tissues an assessment must be made as to the likelihood of damage. If there is considerable pressure within the tissues, multiple small cuts through the skin can be made to allow direct drainage of the fluid. If the fluid is harmful then it can be flushed out through the multiple cuts by using a harmless irrigation fluid such as normal saline.

An alternative method is to inject an enzyme into the tissues which breaks down the natural physical barriers, allowing the fluid to disperse through a larger area of tissue. This should only be done if the fluid within the tissue is harmless. Another possibility is to use locally applied drugs which cause increased blood flow to the area in an attempt to take the fluid away naturally. Despite all these possibilities, there is no universally accepted treatment for this problem in paediatric practice.

Case study: failure to inspect an intravenous cannula causing extensive damage to the back of the hand

His parents brought Christopher, aged five weeks, to hospital. They had noticed for the previous few days that he had been making odd movements which they couldn't explain, but on the day of admission he had had what they recognised as three epileptic fits.

He was admitted to the paediatric ward, blood tests revealed no abnormalities, but as he continued to have intermittent fits it was decided to start him on intravenous anti-epileptic therapy, phenobarbitone. An intravenous cannula was sited in the back of his hand and the first dose of phenobarbitone given successfully. Christopher's hand was then bandaged to protect the cannula.

Christopher stopped fitting but it was decided to continue with maintenance phenobarbitone, which was to be given intravenously for three days. On the third day Christopher began to scream after the phenobarbitone had been injected intravenously by the junior paediatric doctor. Examination of the back of his hand revealed an extensive area of purple skin. Despite attempts at treatment, the skin died and Christopher was left with a large unsightly scar, but also with difficulty in making a fist, as the scarred skin on the back of his hand tethered the tendons to his fingers.

An investigation of the incident revealed that the junior doctor had not followed ward protocol and had not taken the bandage off Christopher's hand to inspect the cannula site before giving the phenobarbitone.

The hospital had no option but to admit liability.

INTRA-ARTERIAL INFUSIONS

The intravenous route is used routinely for all maintenance intravenous fluids and drugs. However, there are occasions when arterial access is necessary. It is more accurate to gain estimation of pH, oxygen and carbon dioxide using arterial blood. Similarly, it is more accurate to measure blood pressure via a cannula in the artery in sick children than using the normal blood pressure cuff. The cannula placed in the artery is kept patent by a slow infusion of fluid that contains an anticoagulant.

There are inherent dangers in using cannulae in arteries. The artery may be punctured, allowing blood under high pressure into the tissues. This can eventually lead to such pressure that the artery collapses, causing lack of oxygen to the tissues beyond the block. The artery itself may go into spasm around the cannula, again causing a lack of oxygen to tissues beyond the cannula, and finally, despite the anticoagulant, clots can form which block the artery completely.

Drugs can be given into the arterial cannula but there are certain drugs that are prohibited because of their damaging effect on the arteries themselves.

The common artery to be used in children is the radial artery at the wrist. Regular inspection of the fingers of that hand is essential. If the finger or fingers become blue or white then the cannula must be removed immediately. Unfortunately, despite removal, recovery of the hand and fingers does not always occur. There have been cases of hands being lost, especially in babies. Such dramatic damage is not necessarily caused by negligence, as long as careful inspection has been undertaken.

Case study: intravenous drug given intra-arterially causing long term growth damage of the forearm

Candice was admitted, aged three months, with difficulty in breathing. She was admitted to the general paediatric ward for observation. It was felt she was suffering from a chest infection and so she received intravenous antibiotics. However, on the third day of admission her breathing became worse and she suffered a respiratory arrest. She was intubated and stabilised on the ward. She already had an intravenous line for the antibiotics, and an intra-arterial line was sited in her right radial artery.

She had to be transferred to the paediatric intensive care unit, which was some 200 yards away, so she was moved in a transport incubator. This is a wheeled incubator which has a ventilator attached to it. During the short transfer she was noticed to be fitting. On arrival at the paediatric ICU she was noted to be intensely blue, not breathing, and her heart rate was dropping. Despite increasing the force of the ventilator, Candice remained blue and her heart rate dropped further. It was decided that the fits must be aborted using intravenous diazepam (Valium). The diazepam was drawn up in a syringe but attempts to infuse the drug were unsuccessful as the intravenous cannula had blocked completely. The paediatrician decided to infuse diazepam into the arterial cannula. Immediately after infusing the diazepam, Candice stopped fitting, became pink and her heart rate became normal. However, her forearm and part of her upper arm became mottled. Infusion of normal saline into the artery did not improve the situation and the forearm remained mottled for the next 48 hours.

When Candice was five years of age it was clear that there had been differential growth between the right and the left arms. The right forearm and hand was considerably smaller than the left forearm and hand, so that the overall arm length was different and asymmetry was obvious to the casual observer.

The claimants argued that the paediatrician had been negligent in using the arterial route for diazepam. When it was recognised that the venous route was blocked, either a new intravenous cannula should have been sited or the diazepam should have been administered rectally.

The defendants argued that Candice was *in extremis* and that further delay may have led to cardiac arrest as well as respiratory arrest. Cardiac arrest is well recognised to cause significant brain damage in children. There was therefore no time to site a new intravenous cannula, especially as success could not be guaranteed. She had concerns about using the rectal route because a child *in extremis* diverts blood away from the guts to essential organs such as the heart and brain. Therefore, absorption may have been delayed, with further delay controlling Candice's seizures. Further, there was no written contra-indication to the use of diazepam intra-arterially. Thus it was entirely reasonable, and in the best interests of Candice, that the arterial route was used.

The expert witness for the claimants asserted that the arterial route was inappropriate. The expert witness for the defendants agreed that normally the rectal or intravenous routes should be used, but in this case the urgency of the situation demanded immediate action. There was no agreement between the two sides. The hospital settled for a modest sum without admitting liability.

CHAPTER 9

ACCIDENTAL INJURY

INTRODUCTION

There are two areas of potential litigation with regard to accidental injury. The first relates to the liability of those who may be partly or wholly responsible for the accident. The second is the consequences of medical treatment. The liability for the accident may be the driver of the car, which may indeed be a parent in the case of children, it may be the driver of another car, or it may be a company or corporation. This may be true, for example, in accidents involving displaced paving stones, missing railings that are the responsibility of the local council, or accidents within private or public buildings such as hospitals or schools. The discussion of such liability is outwith the scope of this book.

Accidental trauma itself can be divided into physical and psychological trauma. Physical trauma is normally the remit of general or trauma and orthopaedic surgeons, but there is frequently an input from medical paediatrics as well.

Psychological trauma frequently falls within the realm of medical paediatrics, as such trauma is often mild or moderate and self-limiting. Only occasionally do the more specialist services need to be involved.

IMMEDIATE EFFECT

Immediate trauma can obviously happen to any part of the body. However, it is equally obvious that trauma to some parts of the body is likely to have more profound consequences than others. Rapid assessment of children who have suffered accidental injury must be sufficiently expert to be able to prioritise the treatment of the sometimes several injuries that children receive, so that those that potentially have the most serious short and long term outcome are treated with the greater urgency and greater priority than those that have lesser long term impact. The approach to the injured child is covered in courses such as PLS (Paediatric Life Support) and APLS (Advanced Paediatric Life Support), which should be attended by all paediatric medical staff, although as yet it is not mandatory.

Head injuries

This is also covered in Chapter 10. The skull is a robust box designed to withstand an impact of considerable force, especially the forehead, which is made of quite thick bone. However, although the skull may not be fractured, there may have been sufficient force to injure the brain, and once the brain becomes injured, it becomes swollen. The swelling of the brain increases the pressure within the skull, which cannot itself expand. If this pressure becomes significantly raised, then the blood supply to the brain may be compromised as the blood vessels collapse secondary to this rise in blood pressure. This then would cause further damage to the brain.

Severe head injuries, such as may result from a road traffic accident, may lead to counter coup injuries. This occurs if the head is moving forward, for example, in a car, and the car stops suddenly as in a road traffic accident. The child may be flung forward and hit his head, either against the dashboard, windscreen or back of the front seats, so the skull stops moving. However, the brain continues moving and collides with the inner surface of the skull, causing damage to the front of the brain. The brain then ricochets and damage is caused to the back of the brain as that part then forcibly contacts the back of the skull. In this sort of injury, a large amount of brain tissue is damaged, causing significant swelling within the brain and subsequent increased intracranial pressure. There therefore needs to be a mechanism for assessing not only the amount of physical damage done in a head injury, but also the amount of neurological damage sustained. There also needs to be a mechanism for assessing the progress or resolution of such neurological damage.

Hospitals should have an algorithm for the investigation of head injuries in children. A commonly accepted algorithm is that all children who have been knocked out need a skull x-ray. If a fracture is noted on skull x-ray then the child should receive a CT scan of the head. The purpose of the scan is to determine whether there is any bleeding within the skull that needs to be stopped, or if there is a need for blood clots to be evacuated in order to reduce the pressure within the skull.

Neurological damage is assessed by the Glasgow Coma Score (qv), maximum score 15. This gives an indication as to the severity of the immediate effect of the head injury but also, by re-applying the criteria for the Glasgow Score, the evolution of the neurological damage can be assessed, thus allowing a decision to be made as to whether any intervention is necessary.

Glasgow Coma Score	4–15 years		<4 years
Best Motor Response	**Score**		**Score**
Obeys verbal command	6	Spontaneous or obeys verbal command	6
Localises pain	5	Localises to pain or withdraws to touch	5
Withdraws from pain	4	Withdraws from pain	4
Abnormal flexion to pain (decorticate)	3	Abnormal flexion to pain (decorticate)	3
Extensor response to pain (decerebrate)	2	Extensor response to pain	2
No response to pain	1	No response to pain	1
Best Verbal Response			
Orientated and converses	5	Alert, babbles, words to usual ability	5
Confused and converses	4	Less than usual words, irritable cry	4
Inappropriate words	3	Cries only to pain	3
Incomprehensible sounds	2	Moans to pain	2
No response to pain	1	No response to pain	1
Eye Opening			
Spontaneously	4	Spontaneously	4
To speech	3	To speech	3
To pain	2	To pain	2
No response to pain	1	No response to pain	1
	TOTAL 3–15		

Any child who has received a head injury that is considered to require in-patient admission should also receive neurological observations. These observations assess the immediate state of the child and, by being applied frequently, assess the neurological stability of the child. These observations assess the degree of consciousness as indicated by response to command, the size of the pupils, the heart rate and the blood pressure.

Increasing swelling of the brain increases the overall pressure within the skull. The only relief valve in the skull is the large exit hole for the spinal canal at the base of the skull. Eventually the base of the brain may be forced through this opening, so called coning of the brain. This is rapidly fatal if not treated with extreme urgency. The signs that this is happening are decreasing level of consciousness, increasing blood pressure and slowing of the heart rate.

There are various options for treatment of raised pressure within the skull that is not due to bleeding. The treatments are designed to reduce the volume of the contents in the brain. A hypertonic solution, such as mannitol, can be infused into the child's veins. This increases the osmotic pressure in the blood vessels, so drawing water out of the brain and effectively shrinking it. This effect can last for several hours, but eventually equilibrium will again be restored and the brain swelling recurs. However, in that interim period there will be some resolution of the traumatic swelling itself. A next step is to intubate and ventilate the child so that the carbon dioxide level drops. This causes constriction of the blood vessels in the brain, so reducing the total volume of the contents within the skull. This effect lasts only 24–48 hours, but may buy precious time. However, there has to be a balance between reducing the size of the blood vessels in the brain against the volume of blood being delivered to the brain in order to keep the brain viable.

The final option is to open a flap of skull so that the brain itself can expand and the pressure within the brain is released.

Case study: fatal head injury: the fault of the pedestrian or the driver?

Kirsten's family decided that they would like to experience an English Christmas and also escape the bitter cold of a Finnish winter. They rented a flat and Kirsten soon met other 14 year olds, with whom she struck up a friendship. She was allowed to go into town with her friends to enjoy some Christmas shopping. Later that afternoon, Kirsten and her friends were walking back home along the main road. Kirsten stopped to post some of her Christmas cards. She got separated from her friends across a side road. She checked the traffic and stepped out, right in front of a car. She suffered a severe head injury where her head smashed into the windscreen. She lost consciousness immediately and was breathing only intermittently. Fortuitously, a general practitioner was passing who had an emergency airway in her car and applied artificial respiration to Kirsten until the ambulance arrived.

The paramedics intubated Kirsten at the scene and she was ventilated throughout the journey to the Accident and Emergency department. Ventilation continued and she was admitted to the neurosurgical ward. A CT scan revealed no acute bleed but extensive damage and swelling in the left tempero-parietal area. It was decided to operate and open a flap of her skull. The pressure within the skull was so intense that part of the brain extruded through the generous skull flap. Unfortunately, it became clear over the next few days that Kirsten was brain dead, and intensive care was terminated.

Kirsten's parents sued the driver of the car for driving without due care and attention. However, there were many witnesses on a busy Saturday afternoon who indicated that Kirsten had automatically looked for traffic coming from the direction she would have anticipated in Finland and did not see the car approaching from the right as she stepped off the pavement. Following advice from counsel the case was discontinued.

Bony injury

The treatment of bony injuries is the remit of the trauma and orthopaedic surgeons. Childhood bony injuries that are treated appropriately rarely run into complications because of the excellent healing powers of children. Negligent or substandard care in paediatric trauma is outwith the remit of this book. Paediatricians may, however, be involved later in injuries that have involved joint dislocation or derangement because of later arthritis.

Soft tissue injuries

Soft tissue injuries are common. They are the result of trips or falls or road traffic accidents when children may suffer quite extensive soft tissue damage. If the trauma occurs in the abdominal area, or in well muscled areas such as the buttocks or the thighs, injuries can be extensive but not include underlying bony damage.

Soft tissue injury to muscles or skin frequently only requires supportive therapy with adequate analgesia. However, trauma to the abdomen may result in damage to the organs within the abdomen. Such damage can sometimes be quite difficult to recognise.

Trauma to the kidneys may occur following a blow to the flanks just below the rib cage. This can occur in contact sports or may be part of a road traffic accident. Blood is lost in the urine, indicating internal haemorrhage within the kidneys. However, unless there is rupture of the kidneys, conservative treatment is indicated and the kidneys heal.

Rupture of the spleen, which can occur in blunt injury to the abdomen, is potentially fatal from haemorrhage into the abdominal cavity. Children whose spleen is ruptured can become shocked from the loss of circulating volume. They become pale. Initially the blood pressure is maintained, but the heart rate rises in order to compensate for the loss of blood within the system. Eventually, however, as more blood is lost, the heart can no longer compensate by increasing the speed of beating and the child's blood pressure drops and, unless recognised, the child will perish.

Case study: misinterpretation of a rash leads to a missed diagnosis of abdominal trauma

Jamie, aged four, woke up and had breakfast with his mother before she went off to her weekend job. He was well and chatted happily to his mother before she left for the day. Jamie's father had worked the late shift at the factory, returning home at 2 am, and was woken by Jamie crying. Jamie had shut his fingers in the door and was crying inconsolably.

The damage to the finger appeared to his father to be only superficial, but Jamie remained inconsolable. Later that morning, his father rushed Jamie into the local Accident and Emergency department as he had lost consciousness. There was little history as Jamie had apparently been perfectly well until losing consciousness. Examination revealed a bruise-like rash over Jamie's abdomen and a clinical diagnosis of meningococcal septicaemia was made. Jamie was shocked, his pulse rate was high, although his blood pressure was maintained, and he received appropriate fluid replacement and was started on appropriate antibiotics. Despite this therapy, Jamie continued to deteriorate and the decision was made to intubate and ventilate. He required maximal support for his blood pressure but this could not be maintained and Jamie died later that evening.

Post mortem revealed a ruptured spleen, and closer inspection of the rash over Jamie's abdomen revealed sharp edges to the rash consistent with heel marks from a shoe. When confronted, Jamie's father confessed that he had been unable to cope with Jamie's inconsolable crying as he was extremely tired from his run of late shift duties, and had stamped on Jamie's abdomen. This caused rupture of the spleen. Jamie's father was jailed for manslaughter as it was accepted that he had not intended to murder Jamie.

Jamie's mother claimed that Jamie died because of medical negligence. The history was not compatible with meningococcal septicaemia, the rash was not compatible and an inadequate clinical examination had been undertaken which had missed the possibility of a ruptured spleen.

The case was not contested.

LONG TERM EFFECTS OF TRAUMA

The long term effects of trauma in childhood can be divided into physical and psychological effects.

Physical effects

Head injury

Severe head injuries can lead to quite devastating brain damage with subsequent effect on the child's IQ. This may result in a degree of learning difficulty that can range from mild to severe.

Epilepsy can occur as a direct result of head injury. It is, however, highly unlikely that a child who receives a head injury but does not lose consciousness will develop epilepsy. Those children that are more likely to develop epilepsy are those that suffer an epileptic seizure as well as a loss of consciousness following the injury. Generally seizures, if they do occur, happen soon after the injury. However, there are cases where seizures have occurred which appear to be related to a head injury several years, even up to 9–13 years, previously. However, only a very small percentage of children who do lose consciousness suffer subsequent seizures and a vanishingly small percentage of those will suffer seizures for the first time several years after the event.

Case history study: head injury causing later epilepsy

Dilip, aged three, was playing in the back of a car that his father was driving. He was not sitting in a baby seat and was not restrained in any fashion. His father lost control of the car in slippery conditions and hit a tree. Dilip was catapulted forwards between the front seats, hit his head on the dashboard and came to rest in the foot well of the passenger seat. After a period of time, and Dilip's father was completely unclear as to how long this period of time was, Dilip started crying. They were taken to the Accident and Emergency department where it was noted that Dilip had a bruise over the right side of his forehead. It was considered that he might well have lost consciousness, which was why he did not cry immediately, so had a skull x-ray which showed no fracture. He was admitted for observation overnight. His neuro-observations were satisfactory but three hours after the accident, Dilip suffered a generalised tonic clonic seizure that lasted less than a minute.

It was considered that this was a post-traumatic seizure and it was decided not to treat with anticonvulsants. Dilip had no further seizures. Eighteen months later, however, Dilip developed generalised tonic clonic seizures, which occurred approximately two or three times per month. He was started on anticonvulsants. An electroencephalogram (EEG brain tracing) revealed an epileptic focus in the right fronto-parietal area of the brain. It was considered by the neurophysiologist that, on the balance of probabilities, this focus was damage caused by the road traffic accident.

Dilip successfully sued his father's insurance company for compensation.

Bony injuries

The bony injuries that are most likely to have long term sequelae are those that affect joints. These can either be secondary to dislocation of the joint, with secondary traumatic arthritis, or those in which there is a fracture to the bones but that fracture involves the joint surface. Children, however, have excellent recuperative powers and so the long term sequelae may be divided into immediate long term and distant long term sequelae. The immediate long term sequelae, for example, the time taken for the fractures to heal and limb mobility to be restored, may last several months or even years, but generally resolve. However, if there is significant disruption to the joint, later adult arthritis is much more common in traumatised joints than in those joints that have suffered no injury.

Case study: long term pain following injury to elbow

Gareth and his mother were out shopping in the centre of town. Most of the town centre was a pedestrian precinct apart from bus lanes. Buses were parked at the end of their route and Gareth and his mother checked that the traffic was clear and stepped out to cross the road. However, they had failed to see a bus coming round the corner. Gareth's mother realised that they were going to be hit and pushed Gareth aside. His right elbow was struck by the nearside wing of the bus, the force of which flung Gareth to the floor. X-ray revealed a non-displaced fracture of Gareth's right humerus involving the surface of the elbow joint. He was treated with a plaster-of-Paris cast and thereafter with a wrist sling. After mobilisation, Gareth had full range of movement of that elbow. He was able to undertake fine motor movements easily and could play computer games without any discomfort. However, he had to give up playing in goal for his school team temporarily as the jarring of the ball against his hand hurt his elbow. He was examined some six months after the event by a paediatrician who reported that Gareth had full, pain-free range of movements in the right elbow and gave an opinion on prognosis that indicated that there should be no ongoing physical sequelae.

Gareth was re-referred to the paediatrician some two years later when he was still having difficulty with playing in goal and picking up heavy objects, both activities causing pain in his elbow.

Re-examination revealed again full pain-free range of movements and also no pain on active movement of the elbow against resistance. Again the paediatrician gave an optimistic prognosis for complete resolution of Gareth's physical discomfort. This did occur three years after the original accident.

Soft tissue injuries

The commonest sequelae to soft tissue injuries are scars if the skin has been disrupted or if there needs to be open reduction of fractures to the limb long bones. Such scars can be quite extensive and may be disfiguring, especially if over the face. Some scar tissue seems to overgrow, so called keloid scarring, in which the scar tissue becomes worse with time compared with the original injury. This is a particular problem in black children. Scarring may also cause decreased function of joints if the joint is pulled in one direction by the contracting scar tissue.

Plastic surgery may be an option in reducing the unsightliness of scars, especially around the face. However, in children who are prone to develop keloid scars, there is no guarantee that the scar produced by the plastic surgeon will not be subject to keloid scarring, so there may be no overall improvement from operative intervention.

Operative intervention is, however, indicated when there is either a loss of, or compromise to, function of joints by releasing scar tissue to improve joint function.

Damage to subcutaneous fat can lead to fat necrosis. This is when the fat tissue undergoes a similar healing process to skin and becomes scarred. There may be quite a hard lump underneath the skin and it may become dimpled as the volume of fat contracts. This may be unsightly but, generally speaking, fat necrosis in children resolves spontaneously, leaving no long term sequelae.

Psychological effects

The psychological effects of accidental injury vary enormously depending on the personality and the maturity of the child, but most importantly, the age of the child. The younger the child, generally the less psychological effect there is. Young children become immediately distressed following pain or shock, but once recovered from the immediate effects seldom suffer any long term sequelae. They may be distressed for several hours after the event, not because they themselves are in pain or scared but because they recognise that their parents are greatly distressed, which in turn distresses the child. In older children, again there is the immediate shock and distress of the accidental injury, but this resolves over several hours as the pain decreases and as the child recognises that they are in a safe environment. However, thereafter there may be panic attacks, daytime flashbacks or nightmares.

Panic attacks

Panic attacks may be brought on by recollection of the incident or by being in environments that are similar to the environment in which the trauma occurred. For example, children may feel very anxious about travelling in a car if they have had an accident whilst in a car. Crossing the road may be difficult for children who have been run over. This was certainly a problem for Gareth. Panic attacks generally decrease in frequency and resolve entirely, but may need months or years for them to disappear entirely.

Occasionally, treatment is required for panic attacks. The immediate treatment is to get the child to breathe in and out into a paper bag. During panic attacks, children ventilate rapidly and get rid of carbon dioxide. This makes them very dizzy and light headed, increasing the anxiety associated with the panic attacks. Re-breathing air in and out of a paper bag maintains a near normal carbon dioxide level, so the secondary physical problems of hyperventilation are avoided. Children are also taught to recognise the onset of a panic attack and learn techniques for avoiding allowing the panic attack to get out of control. With these techniques, children can contain and control the panic attacks until they spontaneously resolve.

Daytime flashbacks

Daytime flashbacks, when the accident or part of the accident or a distorted image of the accident is relived, are common and entirely unpredictable. They are very frightening in that they remind the child of the accident and the child may well need comforting and reassuring when these flashbacks occur.

Again the prognosis is good. The daytime flashbacks gradually decrease in frequency and again, although it is not possible to be precise, generally resolve within several months to a few years after the actual incident.

Nightmares

Anecdotally, it does appear that nightmares can last considerably longer than either the panic attacks or the flashbacks. The nightmares may not be remembered. All that happens is the child wakes up distressed or the nightmares may contain an aspect or an allusion to the accident itself. The nightmares occur unpredictably and sporadically, but again tend to decrease in frequency over the years and eventually will resolve completely.

The psychological sequelae of accidental injury can initially be quite debilitating and socially paralysing in the short term, but almost invariably the prognosis for eventual complete resolution is good.

Case study: psychological sequelae following minor injury

Gareth, the child referred to in the accident with the bus, was 13 years of age when it happened. He did not suffer nightmares following the incident, and occasionally had flashbacks, but he had panic attacks each time he needed to cross the road. When reviewed the first time by the paediatrician, he would only cross the road if his mother was present and would only cross the road if there was no car in sight. If he could see a car moving, regardless of how far distant the car was, he would not cross the road.

This meant that initially his mother had considerable difficulty in getting Gareth to school on time as he had to cross several busy roads during the morning rush hour, and eventually his mother decided to take Gareth to school later in the morning when the amount of traffic had reduced. This continued for some five months after the accident, but slowly Gareth improved to the point where he was able to cross the road with his mother at his mother's command. He was, however, unable to cross the road by himself unless again he could see no moving traffic.

When reviewed two years later, Gareth was able to travel by himself. He did have some anxiety still about crossing the road and would always, if possible, cross by traffic lights and when he could see that the traffic was stationary. However, there had been considerable improvement over the two years and the prognosis for eventual complete resolution was good.

CHAPTER 10

THE NERVOUS SYSTEM

INTRODUCTION

The neurological system is divided into the central, which consists of the brain and spinal cord, and the peripheral, which consists of the nerves to the body and limbs. Medical paediatrics is mainly concerned with the central nervous system, as damage to the peripheral nerves tends to follow trauma or the treatment of trauma so generally is in the domain of the orthopaedic and general surgeons.

HEADACHE

It is not earth shattering to state that headaches are common. It is likely that everyone during their adult life will experience a headache at some point. Most of these headaches, although painful, are inconsequential and most of us anticipate that the headache will be over in a relatively short period of time and is not a pointer to something more serious. The two main types of headache are tension headaches and migraine, and these can normally be differentiated.

Tension headaches

Tension headaches, as the name implies, are often related to stress. The muscles at the back of the neck become tense and this constant tension in the muscles eventually creates a headache. The headache may be as a result of anxiety or tension at the time or, paradoxically, the headache can come on after the anxiety-provoking episode is over and the person relaxes. Headaches can occur at any time of the day and are relieved by sleep. They can occur in clusters, so children might have headaches on several days before they resolve. The parents are often not aware that the child has a headache unless told, in that there is nothing obvious to see when looking at the child.

It is difficult to be precise about the age at which headaches start. The younger child generally suffers from 'tummy aches', and there is no specific age when 'tummy aches' necessarily translate into headaches, but somewhere around the age of seven to nine years children will move on from complaining about tummy aches to headaches. Both usually have the same implication.

They are a physical manifestation of inner tension. Children do not develop abstract thought until the age of seven or eight years, and therefore express all feelings in terms of concrete pain, that is, tummy ache or headache.

The treatment of such tension headaches in the acute phase is normally a mild analgesic, such as paracetamol or ibuprofen. If the headaches persist, which they can do for many months or even many years, then there may be an underlying emotional difficulty, such as bullying at school, tensions within the family, etc.

Migraine

Children suffer from two types of migraine, abdominal migraine and cranial migraine. In exactly the same way that tummy aches precede headaches, abdominal migraine precedes cranial migraine. There is frequently a strong family history of migraine. Up to 70% of children presenting with migraine have a parent who has migraine. Indeed, if there is no family history of migraine, then the diagnosis of migraine in a child, although not impossible, should be approached with caution.

Migraines, be they abdominal or cranial, tend to be relatively infrequent, although they can occur several times a month. There can be very obvious precipitating food factors, such as chocolates, shellfish, strawberries or cheese, but frequently such obvious triggers are lacking. Again, the migraine may be precipitated by tension or stress or may come on after such stress has been relieved, the so called 'weekend migraine'.

In contradistinction to headaches, there are physical changes. The child is deathly pale and so it is obvious when the child is suffering from a migraine. The migraine, similar to adult migraine, can last for several hours and again, like headaches, the migraine is relieved by sleep. On occasion, the migraine can continue through the following day, although sleep is not normally disturbed.

The treatment of migraine can be by prophylaxis, attempting to prevent the migraine in the first place by taking regular daily medication. Once the migraine occurs, however, then analgesia is necessary. In children this may also be a mild painkiller, but some children need specific anti-migraine treatment.

There are no investigations that help one make a positive diagnosis of migraine; it is a diagnosis of exclusion.

HEAD INJURIES

(See also Chapter 9.)

The head is a closed box. Even in younger children, under the age of 18 months, in whom the fontanelle (soft spot) in the skull has not closed, the head is relatively unexpandable. Increases in the volume of the contents of the head, therefore, lead to increasing pressure within the skull. This in turn can lead to worsening damage to the brain, as there is a risk to the brain's blood supply via collapse of small blood vessels by this high pressure.

Direct trauma to the brain

A head injury leads to a relative movement of the brain within the skull. When this happens, the brain impacts against the inner surface of the skull, leading to bruising at that part of the brain. In severe head injuries there may be a so called counter coup injury where the brain hits, for example, the front of the skull and then rebounds and hits the back of the skull because of the force of the injury. This will then lead to damage or bruising both at the front and the back of the brain. Such damage is then followed by swelling, which may affect anything from a small part to virtually all of the brain. The greater the area of brain that becomes swollen, the greater the increase in pressure within the skull, even if there is no overt bleeding.

The increase in pressure within the skull, regardless of cause, can itself lead to increasing damage to the brain cells as the blood supply to the brain is cut off by the increasing pressure of the brain within the skull. The only relief valve, as it were, is at the base of the skull where the spinal cord is attached to the skull, and in extreme cases the brain begins to be forced down through the opening at the base of the skull (foramen magnum): so called coning of the brain. This is extremely serious and will lead to death if not treated with extreme urgency.

Head injuries range from very minor through to severe. It is inappropriate to x-ray or scan every head injury, so an algorithm should be followed to avoid unnecessary investigation, but also to avoid missing potentially treatable problems following head injury.

The skull is really quite tough, especially the forehead, which contains quite thick bone. A minor head injury usually does not lead to any bony problems. However, if the head injury is sufficient to cause loss of consciousness, a skull x-ray should be undertaken and if there is a fracture demonstrated on the skull x-ray, a CT scan of the head should be undertaken to determine whether there is any bleeding within the head. Many children vomit after a head injury, normally as a result of shock. However, vomiting may be caused by increasing pressure within the skull, so all children who have been knocked unconscious or who have vomited after the head injury should be admitted for observation at least. This is not to say that these are the only reasons for admission for observation, but all such children should be admitted.

Once admitted and investigated appropriately, if there is no active intervention, then children should be maintained on neurological observations which, in head injuries of concern, may be undertaken every 15 minutes. As the stability of the patient becomes more obvious, then the head injury observations may be relaxed to every 30 minutes or every hour. The purpose of such observations is to detect quickly any deterioration in the condition of the child, which can then be treated. An objective score is the Glasgow Coma Score (see Chapter 9), which can be used to determine the extent of deterioration of the child. In most cases, children need to be observed for approximately 24 hours and can then be discharged home, with the advice to bring the child back if there is excessive vomiting or if the child becomes drowsy inappropriately, that is, during the day. Both of these can be signs of increasing pressure in the skull.

If there is bleeding within the skull, the child must be referred on to neurosurgeons to determine whether the blood needs to be evacuated. If there is no obvious bleeding, but there is highly increased pressure within the skull, the only alternative is to open a flap of skull bone to relieve the overall pressure within the head.

Haemorrhage

Head injuries can cause an increase in the volume of contents of the brain. This may be via rupture of the blood vessels.

Subdural haemorrhage

If veins are ruptured, then the bleeding tends to be slow and, as the pressure builds up within the skull, the veins, which are thin walled, tend to collapse and stop the bleeding. However, there is still some increase in pressure. This is the typical bleed of shaken baby syndrome.

Shaken baby syndrome

When the baby's head is shaken violently, there is a sheering of blood vessels allowing a collection of blood, commonly over the top of the brain. There may be little, if anything, to see on inspection, so in young children, especially those under the age of two years who are admitted with a so called acute life threatening episode (ALTE) without any obvious cause, a subdural haemorrhage should be considered. An ALTE may be a fit or a period of apnoea (stopping breathing). Retinal haemorrhages (bleeding in the back of the eye) may accompany subdural haemorrhages in shaken baby syndrome.

Case study: lack of appreciation of bruising in a young baby allows further abuse

Samantha was brought to the Accident and Emergency department at the age of eight weeks because her Health Visitor was concerned about some bruising on her legs. The attending doctor elicited the history that Samantha was entirely breast-fed and the parents had refused vitamin K injection. The attending doctor was concerned that the bruising was spontaneous, secondary to a problem with Samantha's clotting. Investigations, however, showed that the clotting was entirely normal and the parents were reassured and Samantha discharged.

At the age of three months, Samantha was admitted from home via a 999 call because she had had a fit. Careful examination revealed no abnormalities at all and so the cause of the fit was unknown. It was decided to undertake a lumbar puncture (taking fluid from the spine), which was heavily blood stained. The lumbar puncture had been difficult, and it was felt that this bloodstaining came from damage to vessels in the spinal canal by the needle.

Samantha had no further episodes, made good progress and was discharged two days later. Two weeks later, Samantha was rushed into the Accident and Emergency department, having stopped breathing at home. She was resuscitated with difficulty. Examination of the retina revealed haemorrhages at the back of the eye. A CT scan revealed not only a large fresh subdural haemorrhage, but also an old subdural haemorrhage. It is likely that the previous admission, when Samantha had a fit, was the time when the first shaking episode had occurred. Sadly she died and her father was tried and convicted for manslaughter.

This case illustrates the difficulties in diagnosis for the medical staff, but emphasises the need for a high index of suspicion of non-accidental injury, especially in young children.

Subarachnoid haemorrhage

Arterial bleeding in the head is much more serious, and unless diagnosed and treated quickly, frequently leads to severe disability or death. Fortunately, rupture of arteries is not common, even in head injuries. The commonest artery to be ruptured is the middle cerebral artery that can be ruptured following a fracture to the temple area of the head. There can be a considerable delay between the injury and the severe effects of the arterial bleed. Even if the child is knocked out by the trauma to the head and the artery is ruptured, consciousness can return for some time before the build-up of blood in the head causes further loss of consciousness.

Case study: missed skull fracture leading to death

Anthony was very proud to have been picked to play cricket for his school under-13 team. He was considered to be an outstanding fielder and was placed at silly mid-on. During the game, his attention wandered and he was caught unawares by a ball coming towards him. He instinctively turned his head and ducked in an attempt to avoid the ball, but it caught him just above his left ear. He was knocked to the ground but did not lose consciousness. He retired hurt and was picked up half an hour later by his parents.

He was complaining of a headache and so was taken to the Accident and Emergency department where, despite having not lost consciousness, he did have a skull x-ray. This was normal and he was allowed home. He went to bed to try to ease his headache and was found dead in bed by his parents five hours later. Post mortem revealed that the middle cerebral artery had been ruptured, which was the cause of death.

The claimants argued that with such a history he should have had a CT scan. The hospital denied this, arguing that he had been appropriately investigated and had had a skull x-ray even though he had not lost consciousness. However, re-examination of the skull x-ray revealed a small linear fracture in the temporal area of the skull which, by the hospital's own protocol, would have necessitated a CT scan of the head. The case was not contested.

EPILEPSY

There are many types of epilepsy, some of which are easily recognisable, such as the generalised tonic clonic fits. These were formally known as *grand mal* epilepsy and are manifest by loss of consciousness, with subsequent jerking of all four limbs. Others may just be short absences, so called simple absences, and others may actually be manifest as a behavioural change, so called partial seizures. Generally speaking, the diagnosis is made on the history, which is virtually always hearsay, the parents either reporting fits that they have seen in their child or reporting what friends of their child have seen. Epilepsy may arise for no obvious reason, or it may be secondary to damage to the head, for example, following a head injury, or very rarely it can be a manifestation of a growth in the brain.

There are few investigations that are helpful in the diagnosis of epilepsy. An electroencephalogram (EEG, brain tracing) may be helpful. However, children can have a normal brain tracing, but still have epilepsy, and some children can have an abnormal brain tracing but not have epilepsy. There are, however, two types of epilepsy which have a very specific abnormality in their brain tracing. Simple absences have a specific three-per-second spike and wave pattern, and infantile spasms, or Salaam fits, have a chaotic brain tracing known as hypsarrhythmia.

Investigating epilepsy

There is little point in undertaking a skull x-ray in epilepsy, in that a tumour in the brain will not show up unless there is calcium within the tumour itself, which is uncommon. However, a brain scan is indicated for fits which are focal, that is, they start and sometimes remain affecting only one area of the body, for example, an arm or a leg or just half the body. Epilepsy is a very rare initial manifestation of a brain tumour, but focal seizures are the type most likely to be caused by a tumour.

Pseudoseizures

Occasionally, fits may either be completely factitious or deliberately staged, so called pseudoseizures. Reporting factitious fits which end up in the child being treated for epilepsy that they don't have, may be part of the so called Munchausen's Syndrome by Proxy. This is a psychological problem of the parents, more frequently of the mother than the father, when illness is manufactured in the child, who is then unnecessarily investigated and treated because of the parent's own problems.

Pseudoseizures are created by the children themselves and may be difficult to distinguish from full seizures. However, generally each time a child has a fit the brain tracing will be abnormal if it is true epilepsy. Having a brain tracing whilst the child has a pseudoseizure will show no change in the brain tracing, indicating that these are not central epilepsy. The exceptions to this are frontal seizures, that is, fits triggered by a discharge in the frontal lobes of the brain. The fits frequently manifest as behavioural changes or abnormalities, and there may not be a discharge on the EEG so they can be extremely difficult to diagnose. It may be necessary to try a course of anticonvulsants to determine whether there is an effect.

Case study: failure to follow guidelines for investigation of epilepsy misses a brain tumour

Ivan presented at the age of six years with fits. His parents gave a clear history that the fits only involved his left arm and his left leg. His brain tracing showed that there was a focus of irritation in the right side of his brain, which would explain the fits. He had a skull x-ray, as this was before CT scans were readily available, which was normal. He was started on anti-epileptic medication that partially suppressed his fits.

Three years later, Ivan's care was transferred to a different consultant who managed to suppress Ivan's fits completely, and after two years being fit-free, the anti-epileptic medication was stopped.

Nine months later, Ivan was referred back by his GP as the fits had re-started. A repeat brain tracing was undertaken, which was similar to the one taken when Ivan was aged six years, and anti-epileptic medication was started again. The fits were less easily suppressed this time but eventually Ivan again became fit-free.

Two years after Ivan had begun to have fits again, he presented in the Accident and Emergency department fitting constantly (status epilepticus). His fits were controlled. He had a CT scan that showed that he had a large tumour in his brain.

The tumour was removed at operation but sadly Ivan suffered considerable brain damage.

The claimants argued that when Ivan presented for the second time he should have had a CT scan. By that time, CT scans were more accessible than when Ivan first presented at the age of six years, and by the time Ivan re-presented it was generally accepted that CT scans were indicated in focal seizures. The case was not contested.

Timing of cessation of epilepsy therapy

Most children grow out of their fits. Some types of epilepsy, such as simple absences, only occur in childhood and normally abate during early teenage years. When a child stops having fits, therefore, it is unclear whether this is just natural history or whether it is because the anti-epileptic medication has been effective. The only way to discover whether a child needs continuing anti-epileptic therapy is to stop that therapy. However, if the therapy is stopped too soon, there is a relatively high incidence of recurrence of the fits. It is now accepted practice that anti-epileptic therapy can be stopped when the child has been fit-free for two years. The anti-epileptic therapy should not be stopped suddenly but should be reduced over a period of months.

There is still a possibility that a child will have a recurrence of fits even after a period of two years without seizures, so some children, as they approach late teenage years and driving becomes a possibility, elect to continue on anti-epileptic therapy to control their fits even if they have had a protracted period fit-free.

Single seizures are in themselves not dangerous to the body in that the brain does not become starved of oxygen. However, status epilepticus, or continuous fitting, can itself cause a lack of oxygen to the brain if not aborted. The major reason, however, for treating epilepsy is not because the seizures themselves are dangerous to the brain, but because having an unexpected seizure may place the child in danger, for example, having a seizure when crossing the road.

Many children do not have a warning, or aura, and therefore certain activities are more safely not undertaken, for example, using high apparatus during PE, riding a bike on roads, and swimming unsupervised. However, supervised swimming and riding a bike around a garden are perfectly acceptable. If a child does have a seizure whilst riding a bike in a traffic-free area, falling off will be painful but would not normally be fatal. Similarly, having a seizure in the swimming baths is not fatal if someone is looking after the child. However, occasionally some children and adults with epilepsy suffer sudden unexplained death. This is unusual, but is related to the epilepsy itself and not related either to cessation of therapy or to the child dying as a consequence of having had a fit in a dangerous environment.

Case study: epilepsy associated sudden death

Jeremy had suffered from generalised tonic clonic fits (loss of consciousness with subsequent jerking of all four limbs) for six years. He had had one period of two years when he had been fit-free and his medication had been reduced and finally stopped. However, a year later he developed seizures again. These appeared to be easily controlled with anti-epileptic therapy, and after 18 months without seizures, Jeremy and his mother persuaded his consultant to withdraw the anti-epileptic therapy rather than wait again for two years. Two months later, Jeremy's father found him dead in the bath just after his 12th birthday.

The claimants argued that the consultant should not have stopped the anti-epileptics early, and that had Jeremy still been on his medication he would not have had a fit in the bath and subsequently drowned.

Observation in the bathroom showed that there was no water around the bath, suggesting that there had been no splashing, and post mortem revealed that drowning was not the cause of death.

The defendants argued that Jeremy had suffered sudden unexpected death and had died immediately and coincidentally in the bath. As drowning was not the cause of death, he must have suffered a sudden catastrophic incident. Stopping the medication would have made no difference to the likelihood of Jeremy suffering sudden unexpected death and, therefore, stopping the medication six months early was not relevant. After taking advice from counsel, the case was discontinued.

TUMOURS

The contents of the skull are divided by a horizontal sheet of tissue into two compartments. This sheet is called the tentorium, and so the compartments are called supratentorial, that is, in the upper part of the skull, and infratentorial, that is, the bottom part of the skull. The supratentorial area contains the cerebrum, or the major centres of the brain for speech, vision and movement, as well as personality. The infratentorial part contains the cerebellum, which is involved in co-ordination of movement.

The commonest site for tumours in childhood is in the cerebellum, or infratentorial area.

Supratentorial tumours

Tumours can occur in the supratentorial area, and the commonest is known as craniopharyngioma. This is actually a benign tumour, but causes immense damage by continuing growth causing local destruction. It is known as benign because it does not metastasise, that is, it does not seed into any other parts of the body. It arises around the nerves from the eyes, so can cause visual problems, normally loss of vision in certain areas of the visual field. It will eventually cause headaches and vomiting by increasing the pressure within the skull, but only once the tumour is quite sizeable.

Infratentorial tumours

Tumours in the cerebellum, or infratentorial area, can cause raised pressure in the skull by two mechanisms. They can either grow and cause pressure by increasing growth, or they can shut off the fluid that circulates from the centre of the brain outwards: cerebro-spinal fluid (CSF). This is produced in the centre of the brain by a leash of blood vessels. If the circulation is stopped, the fluid still continues to be produced and therefore creates enormous pressure in the centre of the cerebral hemispheres in the supratentorial area.

Most tumours are relatively slow growing and so it often takes several months for the diagnosis of a cerebral tumour to be made, as children will often present with rather vague symptoms such as lethargy, walking less well, clumsiness, etc. The role of the secondary paediatrician is to attempt to sort out the very few children with tumours from the many with benign problems. Thus, although rare, the paediatrician should always consider tumours in children displaying unusual symptoms.

Tumours and headaches

The major worry of most parents presenting with children with headaches is that there is a tumour growing in the child's head. The vast, vast majority of children presenting with headaches have an entirely benign explanation, but the basic role of the secondary paediatrician is to try to recognise particular features in children in order to try to identify those children who may have an intra-cerebral tumour.

There is a classical triad of symptoms indicative of the increased pressure within the skull caused by the tumour. These are early morning headaches, effortless vomiting, and papilloedema. Early morning headaches are those that are present immediately on waking; most headaches come on after waking. The reason why the headaches caused by tumours are worse in the morning is that we all breathe in a more shallow fashion during the night and carbon dioxide in the blood rises slightly. This causes dilatation of the vessels throughout the body, including in the brain. If the vessels in the brain dilate, then the volume of blood increases and this increases the pressure within the skull, causing the early morning headache. As breathing reduces the carbon dioxide after waking, then the headache slowly resolves.

Effortless vomiting occurs when there is no preceding nausea or retching; the vomiting is indeed effortless.

Papilloedema is swelling of the nerve head at the back of the eye as it is pushed forward into the eye by the pressure within the skull. However, these features occur late in presentation of a tumour so the paediatrician must be alert to earlier or unusual signs in children.

Paradoxically, the parents who are worried most are those that need to worry least. These are parents who arrive at the Paediatric Outpatients with a child who has had headaches for many months, maybe a year or two years, for which there seems to be no resolution. Although cerebral tumours grow slowly, they do grow and there is now clear evidence that if a child has had headaches for eight months or longer, there is a very low likelihood of it being related to a cerebral tumour, as the tumour would have manifest itself before that time. Therefore, the children who present earlier with headaches are a group that might be looked at more carefully.

The sorts of problems that might alert a paediatrician to the headache being abnormal are the headache waking the child during the night, or a deterioration in the co-ordination of the child. Tension headaches and migraine are relieved by sleep; it is unusual for a child to wake because of pain, so such a child is worthy of deeper consideration.

Most tumours arise in the cerebellum and so can affect co-ordination, producing a tremor, indistinct speech or truncal ataxia. The last is when a child is sitting down but waves gently from side to side. These are signs that there is damage to the cerebellum and that co-ordination is being affected.

An intermittent squint should also alert a paediatrician, in that it can be a sign of increasing pressure within the skull and the nerve to one muscle in the eye gets compressed against the base of the skull, causing a palsy in that muscle. If diagnosis is not made at this time, eventually signs of increased intra-cranial pressure will manifest themselves as the triad mentioned above.

Case study: underinvestigation of unusual headaches and a missed tumour

Michael was a 12 year old, robust, easygoing athlete who competed in many of the school teams. He was very popular, was academically above average and gave the impression of enjoying life generally. His parents were somewhat concerned, therefore, that he suddenly started complaining of severe headaches. These headaches could occur at any time during the day. After the headaches had been going on for two weeks, his parents took him to the general practitioner, who examined him and felt these were just tension headaches. However, a month later, Michael was taken back to the general practitioner because these headaches continued, but also he was now waking up during the night complaining of the headache. His general practitioner reviewed him and examined him, and felt that he deserved an urgent referral to the local paediatric department.

He was reviewed by a senior house officer in paediatrics who discussed Michael with the consultant, who advised that Michael should be observed overnight. Michael was duly admitted, and twice during the night woke up and went to the nurses' station complaining of headache. He was given paracetamol and settled down to sleep thereafter. On the consultant ward round the following morning, he was again examined and a diagnosis of migraine was made. There was no family history of migraine.

Michael was advised to avoid eating chocolate and cheese and was reviewed a month later in Outpatients. He was still complaining of headaches, but was felt to be rather better. However, two weeks later, Michael was referred again by his general practitioner because he was complaining of severe headache and drowsiness. On admission to the paediatric unit, he was noted to be drowsy. His Glasgow Coma Score was reduced at 12 (normal 15) and he was observed overnight. He improved and it was felt that he had had a severe migrainous episode.

Much to Michael's distress, he was dropped from the school cricket team as his fielding, especially his catching, had deteriorated, as did his batting. He also found that he was unable to ride his bicycle safely and he was banned from riding out on the streets by his parents, as he had fallen off his bike several times. Two months later, in Paediatric Outpatients, he was seen again and the diagnosis of migraine confirmed, and it was felt that he was just going through a pubertal growth spurt that had made him clumsy.

Another month passed and Michael's parents were becoming increasingly anxious and insisted on a CT scan, which showed a large posterior fossa tumour. This was removed successfully but Michael had considerable residual neurological problems.

The claimants argued that a diagnosis of migraine should not have been made in the absence of a family history, and in the presence of abnormal night-time waking. They also argued that there must have been concern about

Michael for there to be admission, as a diagnosis of migraine or headache does not warrant an admission. During that admission, Michael had woken up and demonstrated that he had night-time waking secondary to his headache, and both tension headaches and migrainous headaches are relieved by sleep.

The defendants argued that examination had revealed no abnormality when undertaken at his first admission, both by a senior house officer and by a consultant paediatrician, and that on dietary advice, Michael's headaches had improved.

Liability was admitted by the defendants for the penultimate outpatient appointment, when Michael was showing signs of inco-ordination, but as that was only two weeks before the diagnosis was made, it would make no difference to outcome.

The claimants argued that the diagnosis should have been made beforehand at the first admission, and at the latest should have been made by the second admission when Michael was admitted with alteration of consciousness, which is not commonly associated with migraine.

At trial the claimants succeeded in demonstrating negligence. However, it was acknowledged that even had Michael been diagnosed at the first referral, the tumour would have been present and neurological damage would have supervened. Sixty percent of the total quantum was then allowed.

INFECTIONS

Meningitis

Meningitis is an infection of the membranes covering the brain. The brain is enveloped in the innermost lining of the meninges. There is also another layer lining the inside of the skull. There is thus a potential space between these membranes, which is lubricated by cerebro-spinal fluid (CSF).

CSF is produced in the centre of the brain from a leash of blood vessels called the choroid plexus, which are in cisterns in the brain called lateral ventricles. The fluid produced in the lateral ventricles flows through channels to the centrally-placed third ventricle, through a narrow aqueduct of Sylvius into the fourth ventricle, and then out over the surface of the brain and down the spinal column. Meningitis affects these coverings of the brain, and does not normally affect the brain itself.

There are three broad common categories: bacterial, viral and tuberculous meningitis. Although tuberculosis is caused by a bacterium, it needs different treatment from the others and so is categorised separately.

Bacterial meningitis

The incidence of bacterial meningitis is reducing rapidly now. There are three main organisms: *Neisseria meningitidis* (*Meningococcus*), *Haemophilus influenzae* and *Streptococcus pneumoniae*.

There will be a significant reduction in the amount of meningococcal meningitis now that the *Meningococcus* vaccine is being universally administered. However, there are three strains of *Meningococcus:* A, B and C. Although C is the commonest, and that is the one against which the vaccine is active, it is still possible to have meningococcal disease from A and B.

Haemophilus influenzae has virtually vanished now that the Hib vaccination is given to all infants. This means that bacterial meningitis will eventually be pneumococcal, which in fact is quite rare.

Diagnosis in children over the age of 18 months is usually fairly obvious. The child complains bitterly of a headache, the neck is very stiff from irritation and inflammation, and there is photophobia (dislike of light). With that classic combination, a lumbar puncture is taken which will reveal pus cells and probably bacteria in the CSF itself. A lumbar puncture involves a child lying or being held on its side whilst introducing a needle into the lower part of the spinal column and removing CSF. Treatment is with the appropriate antibiotics.

In infants less than 18 months, there may be much softer signs such as lethargy, irritability and refusal to feed. These are not specific to meningitis at all and can occur in any form of infection. There is, therefore, a very low threshold to undertake a lumbar puncture in children under 18 months, and especially in children under a year who have an infection as evidenced by a raised temperature but the source of the infection can not be detected.

Viral meningitis

Viral meningitis can be caused by several different viruses and is not particularly severe. It causes the same sort of triad of problems with headache, neck stiffness and photophobia in older children. Lumbar puncture is often clear but will show some white cells, tending to be slightly different white cells. The child recovers well and there is no treatment.

Tuberculous meningitis

Tuberculous meningitis is rare in the UK, although there is a slowly increasing number of children contracting tuberculosis in the UK. The onset of symptoms is much more insidious, with headaches, general lethargy, but nothing quite so aggressive as normal bacterial meningitis. Usually, tuberculous meningitis accompanies a tuberculous infection elsewhere in the body, usually in the lungs.

Lumbar puncture shows a very high level of pus cells in the CSF and treatment is with prolonged antitubercular antibiotics.

Encephalitis

Encephalitis is caused by viruses and is a direct invasion of the brain tissue. It can occur after most of the viral childhood illnesses such as measles, mumps or chicken pox. It often occurs 10 days to two weeks after the acute infection itself and can cause a variety of symptoms. These may include ataxia (staggering gait), headaches and odd behaviour. Generally speaking, however, the outlook for viral encephalitis is good and there is no specific treatment. The exception to this rule, however, is herpes encephalitis.

Herpes encephalitis

This is caused by *Herpes hominis* Type I, the virus that causes cold sores. This can cause a necrotising destructive encephalitis and, unless treated early and effectively, has a high incidence of neurological damage if survival occurs, but it is often fatal. Unfortunately, there are no classical symptoms of herpes encephalitis. There may be a history of cold sore either in the child itself or, more often, in a relative or adult. Symptoms include altered consciousness, fits, hallucinations, headaches or bizarre behaviour. Herpes is treatable and the treatment is effective, at least in reducing the amount of neurological damage, so there must be a high index of suspicion. It may well be appropriate to investigate and treat the child with acyclovir whilst awaiting results.

Herpetic encephalitis is a haemorrhagic encephalitis, so there will be blood in the CSF on lumbar puncture. However, one of the difficulties is being confident that the technique of the lumbar puncture was perfect, that is, that the blood within the CSF is not due to the local trauma by the needle.

The classical CT scan finding for herpes encephalitis is an area of abnormality in one of the temporal lobes of the brain.

Blood and CSF can be analysed for herpes by PCR (polymerase chain reaction) which looks for the genes of the herpes virus which are present even if the herpes virus itself cannot be grown.

The outcome for herpes encephalitis is dependent on the speed with which it is treated. The earlier the treatment is instituted with acyclovir the better the outcome. Delays allowing seizures or altered consciousness to occur generally have a poor outcome. Once treatment is started and either the diagnosis is proven or there is a high index of suspicion, then acyclovir should really be continued for 14 days to prevent recrudescence of the infection. However, despite an early diagnosis and adequate treatment, herpes encephalitis can leave children with neurological damage.

Case study: early cessation of treatment allowing recrudescence of herpes encephalitis

Duane became rather lethargic at home, refused to eat and appeared to his mother to have a temperature. She took him to the GP who was unsure of the cause of the temperatures, so referred him to the local hospital. A careful history was undertaken and investigations, including lumbar puncture and a blood culture, were taken.

The lumbar puncture did show blood in the CSF but it was felt that this was due to trauma, and it was decided to observe Duane overnight. However, during that night he became more drowsy, continued with a temperature and had a generalised seizure. The results of the CSF were reviewed. It showed no evidence of meningitis, merely blood in the fluid. However, it was decided to start treatment with acyclovir.

Duane appeared to improve on acyclovir but five days later the herpes PCR came back as negative, so it was decided to stop acyclovir and discharge Duane home.

Five days later, Duane was re-admitted with seizures and a fever. This time a CT scan of the brain was undertaken, showing a lesion in the temporal lobe. He was restarted on acyclovir that was continued for 10 days. Unfortunately, Duane suffered considerable neurological damage and was left with severe learning difficulties.

The claimants argued that acyclovir should have been started as soon as Duane was admitted, and that the acyclovir should have been continued for 10 days as a minimum. There was a recognised false negative reporting for herpes PCR in the presence of bloody CSF, pyrexia, and altered consciousness so there was no indication to stop acyclovir.

The defendants argued that Duane was admitted with no signs of encephalitis. It was admitted that the CSF was bloody but that could have been due to trauma, as some 40% of all lumbar punctures are bloody. Therefore, it was reasonable to observe and that acyclovir started on the second day of admission was the earliest that it could have been anticipated. Although acyclovir was stopped earlier than recommended, the PCR was negative and that Duane's present learning difficulties were related to his acute episode in the first 24–48 hours of the disease.

The claimants produced evidence that there was a recognised false negative result with herpes PCR and therefore a decision to stop medication on such a result was inappropriate, but accepted that there was no overwhelming indication to start Duane on acyclovir on admission.

The judge found for the claimants, indicating that, in a child with altered consciousness, a haemorrhagic CSF and pyrexia for no obvious reason, then it is appropriate to treat with acyclovir and, once acyclovir is instituted, then it should be continued for the appropriate length of time. The second episode was related to a recrudescence of the herpes, which was at least a factor in producing worsening neurological symptomatology in Duane. However, it was accepted that 24 hours after Duane's admission was the appropriate time to start acyclovir and by that time, neurological damage may have occurred. 80% of the total claim was allowed.

CHAPTER 11

THE CARDIOVASCULAR SYSTEM

INTRODUCTION

Normal blood flow

The cardiovascular system includes the heart and all the blood vessels that ramify throughout the body; it is traditionally divided into two sides. The left side of the cardiovascular system refers to the arterial side, containing oxygenated blood; the right is the venous side, containing deoxygenated blood. The left side of the heart pumps oxygenated blood round the body. The right side of the heart collects the venous, or deoxygenated, blood from the body and pumps it through the lungs. These two systems, therefore, work in series, with each red blood cell starting from the left side of the heart, traversing the blood vessels of the body, back to the right side of the heart, through the lungs and then back again to the left side of the heart.

Figure 1: Blood flow through the heart

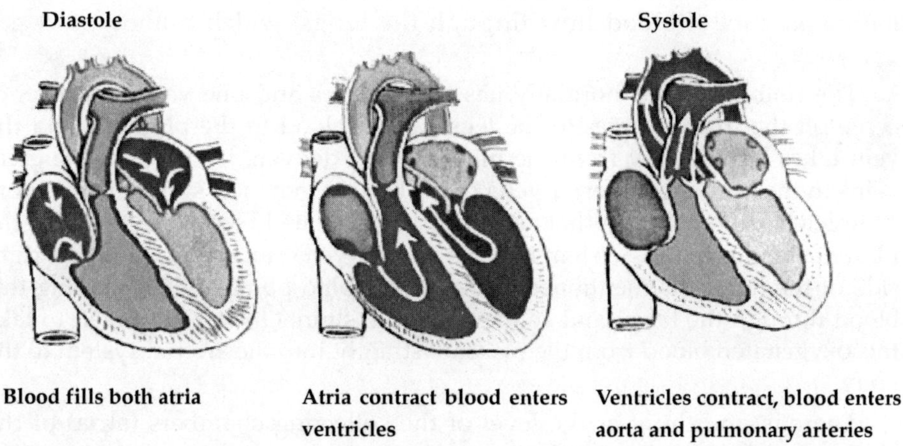

The major oxygen-carrying blood vessels are called arteries. As these divide and get smaller, they become arterioles and these again divide to become capillaries. These are minute blood vessels where gas exchange occurs throughout the body. Oxygen is given up by the red blood cells in the capillaries, and carbon dioxide is taken into the blood stream. After this gas exchange, the capillaries coalesce to become venules, or small veins, and these then again coalesce to become veins, and eventually become the great veins, which return blood to the heart. The only connection, therefore, between the arterial vascular system and the venous vascular system is via the capillaries.

Abnormal blood flow

There may be abnormal flow of blood, either from the arteries to the veins or from the veins to the arteries, and these are called shunts. Blood can be shunted either in the heart, in such conditions as hole in the heart, or between arteries and veins. These are always abnormal and cause abnormalities in blood flow and gas exchange. If oxygenated blood moves directly from the arterial system into the venous system, this is called a left to right shunt. If from the venous system to the arterial system, this is called a right to left shunt.

CARDIOVASCULAR CHANGES AT BIRTH

Fetal circulation

The organ of gas exchange in the fetus is the placenta (afterbirth), not the lungs. The lungs are full of fluid, and therefore there is no point in having large amounts of blood flow through the lungs, which cannot affect gas exchange.

The umbilical cord normally has two arteries and one vein. The arteries come off the main arteries to the legs, taking blood to the placenta, and the vein takes blood away from the placenta and delivers it to one of the great veins in the body: the inferior vena cava. The oxygenation system is therefore completely different from that after birth. Oxygenated blood is taken from the placenta by the venous system into the inferior vena cava and back to the right side of the heart. As mentioned above, there is no point in then sending this blood through the lungs and so there are two shunts from right to left to take this oxygenated blood from the placenta straight into the arterial system to the body.

There is one shunt at the level of the collecting chambers (atria) of the heart, whereby blood comes back to the right atrium and is pumped straight across to the left atrium, into the left ventricle, and then out through the aorta. The other shunt is between the main artery to the lungs, the pulmonary artery, and the aorta, through a connection called the ductus arteriosus.

Figure 2: Patent ductus arteriosus

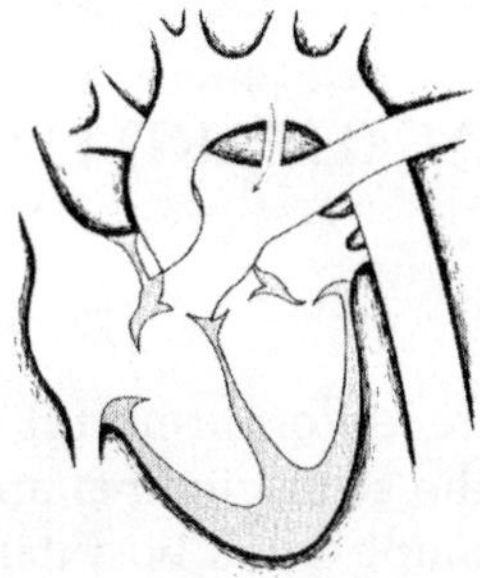

This again means that any blood pumped by the right ventricle preferentially ends up in the aorta. In order for this system to work, there must be a pressure gradient, and so in the womb the right side of the heart pumps at a higher pressure than the left side of the heart so that blood can flow from the right atrium to the left atrium and from the pulmonary artery to the aorta.

Postnatal circulation

Once birth occurs, gas exchange via the placenta is cut off and the lungs must work immediately as the organ of gas exchange. There are, therefore, major changes that occur at the time of birth. The first breath a baby takes generates a large negative pressure. This opens up the lungs and forces air into the millions of little air pockets within the lungs. This expansion of the lungs immediately causes the pressure on the right side of the heart to drop to a pressure lower than that on the left side of the heart. This has the effect of preferentially forcing blood from the right side of the heart into the lungs, where oxygenation can occur. This blood then returns to the left side of the heart and is pumped through the body. Immediately after birth, the closure of the hole between the right and left atrium, the foramen ovale, occurs. The hole is more like a flat valve, so that as the pressure on the left side builds up, it shuts the flap of tissue over the hole between the two chambers.

The increase in oxygen level causes the ductus arteriosus, the shunt between the pulmonary artery and aorta, to close, a closure which becomes an irreversible anatomical closure over the next few days. These changes create a cardiovascular system that can sustain life outside the womb.

The right side of the heart has been at a higher pressure than the left side within the womb. The musculature on the right side of the heart is therefore quite thick, and it takes several weeks for complete adjustment to occur so that the pressure on the right side of the heart drops to normal childhood and adult levels. This slow change is relevant when discussing the appearance and timing of heart murmurs (noises caused by abnormal flow of blood in the heart).

CARDIAC (HEART) LESIONS

Antenatal diagnosis

All pregnant women who receive antenatal care undergo ultrasound scanning. The resolution of the scan pictures and the sophistication of the techniques of ultrasound scanning in all hospitals are such that major heart defects should be detected antenatally. The precise diagnosis of the cardiac abnormality may not be determined in district general hospitals, but the level of detail achievable with the new scan machines should allow ultrasonographers in district general hospitals to determine whether there is a cardiac lesion within a particular fetus. These women are then referred to tertiary centres, where the fetus will undergo a detailed scan by a paediatric or perinatal cardiologist. In this way, the majority of severe cardiac abnormalities are known about before birth.

There is, however, a natural failure rate with ultrasonography so that there are still heart lesions, especially the more subtle heart lesions, that are not picked up at birth. It is therefore important that there are screening procedures in place to try to pick up heart defects in young babies, infants and children.

CARDIAC LESIONS: CATEGORISATION

The broad categorisation of heart defects is into acyanotic, or pink, and cyanotic, or blue. As mentioned above, there are two forms of abnormal shunting of blood, one from the left (arterial) system to the right (venous) system, the basis for pink babies. The other is from the right (venous) system to the left (arterial) system, causing blue babies.

Pink babies

In acyanotic heart lesions, either there is a problem with the valves of the heart, or a narrowing of the major blood vessels such as coarctation of the aorta, or oxygenated blood is pumped from the left (arterial) side into the right (venous) side. In these cases, normal oxygenated blood is pumped through the arterial system throughout the body, as well as abnormally straight from the arterial system to the venous system. The child therefore looks pink, because the blood coursing round the arteries and arterioles is pink and oxygenated. Confusingly, coarctation of the aorta can either be cyanotic, if the narrowing is intense (Fig 3a), or acyanotic, if the narrowing is not so tight (Fig 3b).

Figure 3a: Coarctation of the aorta: intense

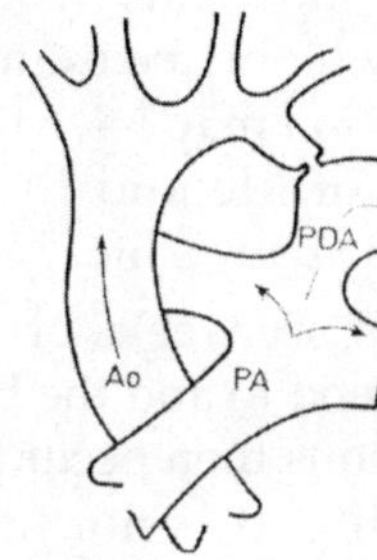

Figure 3b: Coarctation of the aorta: acyanotic

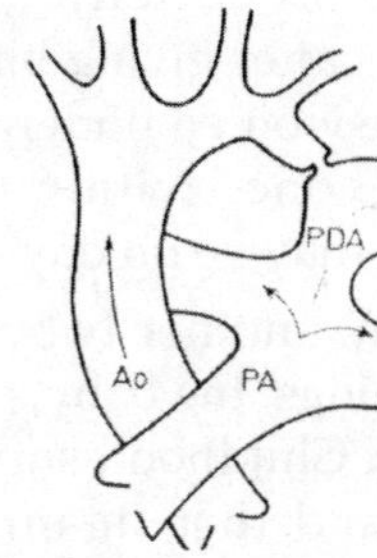

Key:
Ao = Aorta
PA = Pulmonary Artery
PDA = Patent Ductus Arteriosus

Blue babies

Cyanotic cardiac lesions occur when the shunt is from the right (venous) side, when deoxygenated blood is pumped directly into the left (arterial) system. In this case, the blood in the arterial system in the body is both oxygenated and deoxygenated. Deoxygenated blood is 'blue', and so the child looks blue. This is particularly noticeable in the lips and tongue. It is, of course, important to differentiate between a child who looks blue because they are cold, so they have blue fingers, blue tip of the nose and are blue around the lips – this is known as peripheral cyanosis, as opposed to the child who actually has deoxygenated blood in his or her arteries, when the child has blue lips and a blue tongue, so called central cyanosis.

Blue babies, that is, those with a right to left shunt, a cyanotic heart problem, should be picked up at birth, but not all cardiac abnormalities which cause blue babies present immediately at birth. The babies may turn blue months later. Babies with acyanotic, or pink, cardiac defects will look entirely normal at birth. There are, therefore, screening times during which the babies' and infants' hearts should be listened to, to determine whether there are abnormal noises emanating from the heart.

SCREENING FOR CARDIAC LESIONS

The first examination is shortly after birth, normally within the first 24 hours of life. However, significant changes occur at this time in the cardiovascular system, so murmurs which are heard later on, maybe at six weeks of life or even later, may not be present at all in the first day or so of life. It is, therefore, not necessarily negligent if a murmur is heard at six weeks of life but not heard during the first examination.

The pressure on obstetric beds now is such that many women leave hospital six hours after giving birth, so the babies will only be examined once in hospital. Those women undergoing caesarean section may have their babies examined twice, once within the first 24 hours of life and then once at discharge, which may be on day four or day six of the baby's life.

There is, then, another baby-screening check at six weeks of age when, amongst other things, the baby's heart must be listened to and the baby's hips must be checked. Childhood surveillance examinations then occur at 18 or 24 months of life, and then again at 36 months of life. It is not uncommon, therefore, for murmurs to be picked up at these childhood surveillance examinations. Clearly, such murmurs can be heard or picked up at any other time if children are taken along for incidental reasons, such as a cold or cough, when the chest is listened to.

ACYANOTIC CARDIAC LESIONS

By far the commonest type of heart lesion is acyanotic. This produces pink infants with a shunt that goes from the left, or arterial, side to the right, or venous, side.

The innocent murmur

The commonest heart murmur heard is a so called innocent cardiac murmur. This murmur is frequently picked up by the general practitioner, either as an incidental finding in a child who is taken along for another chest problem, such as a cold or cough, or at the 36-month check. The child is perfectly well, and has no symptoms that may indicate an abnormal heart, such as breathlessness or a poor exercise tolerance. Even when the parents have been told that their child has a heart murmur, which normally creates enormous anxiety, the parents cannot notice anything abnormal about their child.

The innocent cardiac murmur is so called because there is no structural abnormality with the heart. What is heard is the rush of blood through a normal heart because of the flow of blood around the muscles within the heart. There are certain features to the added heart noise, or murmur, that must be true. There are two phases when listening to a heart. There is the so called first heart sound, diastole, which is the noise of the valves between the collecting chambers and the pumping chambers closing: the mitral and tricuspid valves. There is then a period called systole, when blood is pumped out via the pumping chambers into the main arteries to the body and to the lungs. The second set of valves, the aortic and pulmonary, then shut, producing the second heart sound. There is then a quiet period when filling of the collecting chambers occurs before the first heart sound, diastole.

An innocent murmur must occur in systole; it cannot occur in diastole. It must occur in the middle of systole and must not continue throughout systole. Commonly, the timbre of the murmur changes depending on the position of the child. It is often more obvious when the child is lying down, and may become quieter or even disappear when the child is standing up.

Innocent murmurs may be intermittent, and they may be more obvious when the child is unwell with a temperature, so the heart is pumping more quickly. They may also be more obvious in women during pregnancy. Frequently, however, these murmurs disappear as the child gets older and goes into adolescence. At this time, the chest wall becomes thicker, the heart rate becomes slower, and so the murmur disappears. If the secondary care paediatrician is convinced that an innocent murmur is the diagnosis, then all that is needed is reassurance to the parents that the child's heart is entirely normal and no special precautions are necessary.

Ventricular septal defect

The commonest acyanotic abnormality is a ventricular septal defect (VSD), a 'hole in the heart'. This is a hole in the dividing membrane between the left pumping chamber of the heart and the right pumping chamber of the heart. In the womb, when the right side of the heart is at a higher pressure, blood will move from the right side of the heart to the left. At birth, as the pressure on the right side drops, then there may be either no or little movement of blood either way as the pressure between the two chambers is fairly similar. It is not until the pressure on the right side of the heart drops that significant volumes of blood will be pumped from the left pumping chamber to the right pumping chamber. It is not unusual, therefore, for a VSD to be missed at birth because no murmur will be obvious. However, it should be obvious by six weeks of age, the first community-based heart screening examination for babies.

Oxygenated blood is pumped from the left side to the right side of the heart. The child is therefore pink and does not suffer from any lack of oxygen going to the tissues. However, if there is a large volume of blood moving from the left pumping chamber to the right pumping chamber, then the left pumping chamber needs to work harder to get the normal volume of blood to the body. If this is excessive, then the heart will go into failure, as it is unable to keep up with the demand. This is unusual. Generally speaking, there is a modest movement of blood from the left to the right and so the left pumping chamber can cope, both with this shunt and also with moving blood around the body. 90% of these holes in the heart will close spontaneously in the first year of life, so operative intervention is resisted and will only be undertaken if the heart goes into failure which cannot be controlled by medical treatment.

Figure 4: Ventricular septal defect

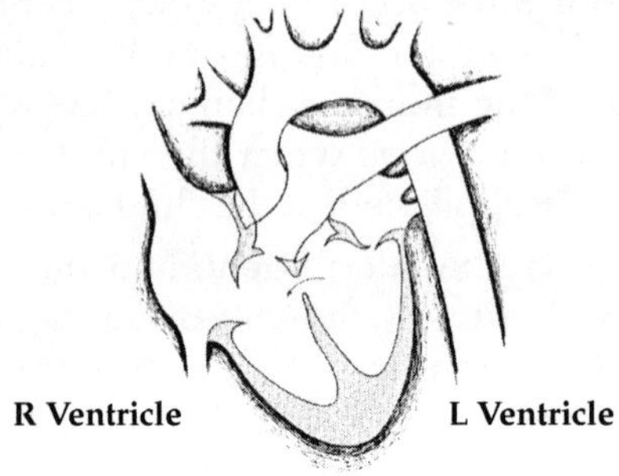

The classical heart murmur of a VSD is a pancystolic murmur. This is when the noise of the murmur covers the whole of the systole period. However, referral to a paediatric cardiology centre for definitive diagnosis is advisable.

Atrial septal defect

Another common acyanotic heart disease is a hole in the heart between the two collecting chambers, atrial septal defect (ASD). Movement of blood from left to the right occurs during the filling stage, that is, diastole. The collecting chambers are at a relatively low pressure, so blood flow is slow and no murmur is heard during diastole. However, there is an increased volume of blood going from the right collecting chamber to the right pumping chamber and out into the lungs because of this shunt. There is, therefore, a heart murmur during systole, that is, the pumping period, because a large amount of blood has to get out quickly through the pulmonary valve and this causes turbulence and noise. Again, referral to a tertiary centre for confirmation is recommended.

Figure 5: Atrial septal defect

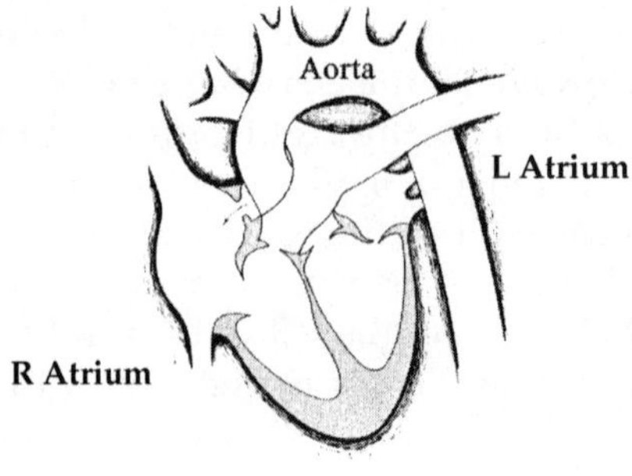

There are many and varied causes of acyanotic heart lesions and this book is not meant as a substitute for a medical textbook. The main thrust, however, is that if there is any doubt in the mind of the secondary care paediatrician with regard to heart abnormalities, referral to a tertiary paediatric cardiology centre is mandatory.

CYANOTIC CARDIAC LESIONS

Cyanotic heart disease is much less common than acyanotic heart disease. However, generally speaking it is more serious than acyanotic heart disease, as deoxygenated blood mixes with oxygenated blood in the body, reducing the amount of oxygen reaching the tissues.

Heart or lungs?

Any blue baby presenting to a district general hospital should be investigated to determine whether a heart or a lung problem is causing the cyanosis. These are the organs that affect either the amount of oxygen getting into the blood, that is, the lungs, or the way the blood is pumped, that is, the heart. Rarely, children have 'blue' blood that relates to an abnormality whereby the blood cells cannot carry much oxygen and therefore do not change from blue to pink. This, however, is very uncommon.

The site of the abnormality, that is, whether in the heart or the lungs, is determined by a nitrogen washout test. In this test, the level of oxygen in the blood is tested with the child in air; it is then re-tested after the child has been breathing 100% oxygen for several minutes. If the oxygen level in the blood stays the same, it suggests the problem is in the heart. If the oxygen level in the blood rises considerably, that suggests the problem is in the lungs. This test therefore allows some differentiation between the causes and allows appropriate referral, if necessary.

There are two relatively frequent types of cyanotic heart disease. The commoner is called Fallot's tetralogy.

Fallot's tetralogy

This is a combination of narrowing of the pulmonary valve, the main valve to the lungs; an overriding aorta, that is, an aorta that sits between the left and right pumping chambers instead of coming off only from the left pumping chamber; a ventricular septal defect, that is, a hole in the heart between the two pumping chambers; and right sided hypertrophy, that is, thickened muscle in the right pumping chamber.

This tetralogy frequently does not present at birth. The time of presentation depends on the degree of narrowing of the pulmonary valve. If the valve is critically narrowed, then the baby will be blue at birth as very little blood will get to the lungs, and because of the hole in the heart, the blood from the right side of the heart will enter the aorta. If, however, the narrowing of the pulmonary valve is modest, then reasonable amounts of blood will flow through the lungs and become oxygenated. It is only when the pressure in the right side of the heart, working against a narrow valve, gets to a point where the pressure in the right pumping chamber exceeds the pressure in the left pumping chamber that deoxygenated blood will be shunted straight into the aorta, and the child will become blue. Thus a child with Fallot's tetralogy may well not present at birth, but will usually present within the first year of life.

Figure 6: Fallot's tetralogy

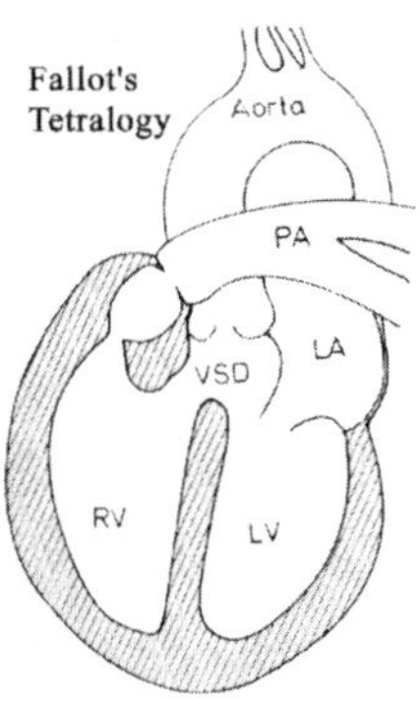

Key:
PA = Pulmonary artery
VSD = Ventricular septal defect
LA = Left atrium
RV = Right ventricle
LV = Left ventricle

Transposition of the great vessels

The other relatively frequent cyanotic heart disease is transposition of the great arteries. In this situation, the heart and the vessels coming out of the heart have been switched, as it were, 180°, with the aorta coming from the right pumping chamber and the pulmonary artery from the left. In this case, the blood coming out of the left side goes to the lungs and the blood coming out of the right side goes to the body. This means that there are two blood circuits in parallel, rather than in series. For example, a red blood cell in the left pumping chamber would go into the lungs and come back via the left collecting chamber to the left pumping chamber again. A red blood cell in the right pumping chamber would go into the body and then back to the right collecting chamber and again into the right pumping chamber. There is therefore no opportunity for blood to be oxygenated, and affected babies are blue at birth.

Figure 7: Transposition of the great vessels

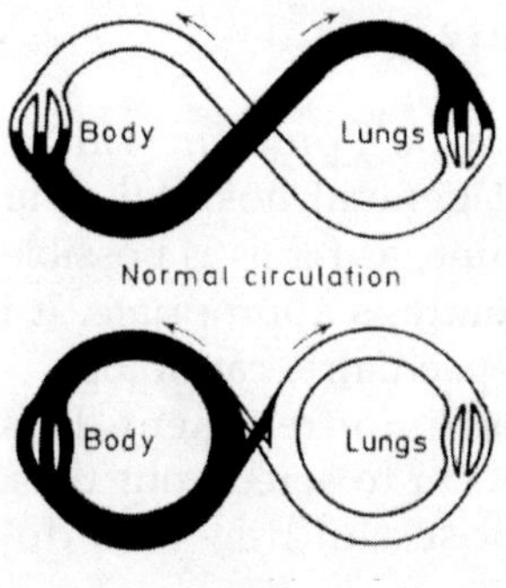

Survival occurs in the short term because of the naturally occurring shunts between the collecting chambers and through the ductus arteriosus.

The main way in which mixing of blood can occur to allow some oxygenation in the body is through the ductus arteriosus. If this shuts because oxygen levels increase, then the baby will succumb rapidly. Urgent referral is therefore required to a cardiac centre. The baby needs to be transported with an infusion of a drug to keep the ductus arteriosus open, which is the baby's only lifeline until he reaches the cardiac centre.

Figure 8: Transposition of great vessels

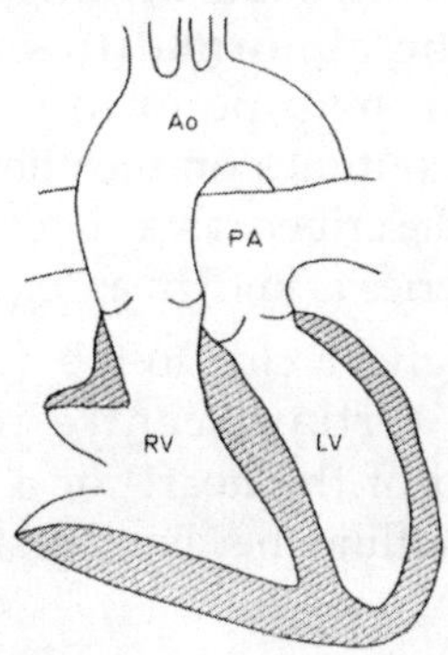

There are again many variations of cyanotic heart problems in children. The secondary care paediatrician is not necessarily expected to make a precise diagnosis, but is expected to recognise cyanosis, to determine whether this is heart or lung in origin, and to communicate with the tertiary centres in order that appropriate treatment is instituted rapidly so the baby or infant can be transported safely until definitive treatment can be undertaken at the tertiary centre.

REFERRAL PATTERNS AND ONGOING CARE

General patterns of care

If a GP feels that there may be a problem with a child's heart, the appropriate referral is to the district general hospital. The role of the secondary care paediatrician is to determine, as far as is possible, whether onward referral to a tertiary cardiological centre is appropriate. It is inappropriate for all heart murmurs to be sent to a paediatric cardiology centre. Innocent murmurs are very common and require no treatment. It is, therefore, the role of the secondary care paediatrician to screen out those children who do not need tertiary care, so that those children who do require tertiary care have appropriate access to it.

There is no universally agreed investigation of children in whom the secondary care paediatrician feels the diagnosis clinically is innocent murmur. Some paediatricians will use their clinical skills only, and reassure the family that all is well. Others may undertake a chest x-ray and electrocardiogram (ECG). These two investigations will be entirely normal. However, although the fact that they are normal is comforting, it does not necessarily rule out the possibility of a structural defect within the heart. They cannot therefore be relied on to make a definitive diagnosis of innocent murmur, hence the variation in approach.

If, however, the district general hospital paediatrician feels that the murmur is abnormal, then the base-line investigations would be a chest x-ray and an ECG. There may be abnormalities in either or both of these investigations which would help point to the diagnosis. There are, for example, characteristic heart outlines on the chest x-ray. The heart in Fallot's tetralogy on chest x-ray is described as a 'boot shaped' heart. The heart in transposition of the great arteries is known as 'egg on its side'.

The ECG may also help give a clue to the diagnosis. However, definitive diagnosis rests with the tertiary centre if there is any doubt. An echocardiogram (ultrasound of the heart) or a cardiac catheterisation (dye introduced into the heart to outline the chambers) will give the diagnosis.

Shared care

Simple cardiac lesions require intermittent visits to the tertiary centre only, with much of the care being undertaken by the district general hospital. Virtually any structural abnormality, with the exception of an atrial septal defect, will require the child to take antibiotics if undergoing a procedure that may allow bacteria into the blood stream. The commonest procedures will be dental. This will not be just an oral hygiene visit, but if there is major dental work such as extraction or work that involves bleeding, then the child should have antibiotics. The reason for this is that if there is a structural lesion in the heart, bacteria within the blood stream have a tendency to lodge on to the structural abnormality and this can cause a low-grade, but destructive, infection of the heart structure itself (subacute bacterial endocarditis).

Complex cardiac lesions may also require shared care if there is a significant distance between the child's home town and the tertiary paediatric cardiology centre. Many, if not most, of the decisions regarding treatment and change of treatment may well be undertaken by the cardiology centre, but monitoring will be undertaken in the district general hospital. Therefore there needs to be clear and good communication between the two paediatric departments so that the local district general hospital is fully aware of the latest treatment that the child is on, and any complications that may be anticipated. In this way, the tertiary centre is used efficiently so that it is only used by children who need tertiary care. Most care is undertaken locally, with less disruption to family life, but there is a 'lifeline' to the paediatric cardiology centre.

Complex cardiac abnormalities frequently demand complex surgery and, indeed, multiple surgery, a detailed knowledge of which is completely outwith the skill of the local district general hospital paediatrician. Such paediatricians are not expected to know details of individual cardiac procedures, nor are they expected to know details about all of the possible complications that may emanate from the structurally abnormal heart, and also from the operated structurally abnormal heart. However, the role of the district general hospital paediatrician is to determine when the child with a cardiac lesion is in trouble and that care in the district general hospital is not appropriate. At this point, rapid communication must be established with the cardiology centre and, if necessary, local treatment instituted before transfer down to the paediatric cardiology centre. Thus, the district general hospital paediatrician acts as a safety net for children with complex cardiac lesions without necessarily knowing the intimate details of all the potential problems the child may face.

Case study: failure of diagnosis and failure of communication in an unfamiliar child with a complex cardiac abnormality

Darryl was born with a complex heart problem. This necessitated several operations on his heart in the major children's heart unit that was 60 miles away from his home. Eventually, it was considered that his heart condition was stable following the construction of a conduit outside his heart, the result of the so called Fontan's procedure. He was seen in Outpatients every six months at the central heart unit and did not attend his local district general hospital. Initially the cardiologist sent letters both to Darryl's GP and to the local hospital consultant. However, there was a change of cardiologist and no further letters were sent to the local hospital consultant.

When Darryl was 10 years old he developed gastroenteritis with copious vomiting and diarrhoea. His mother called the GP, who saw Darryl at home and noted that he had a very irregular heart rate. The GP checked his own records and noted that each time Darryl had been to Outpatients the cardiologist had noted that Darryl's pulse was regular. The GP himself contacted the medical staff at the heart unit who advised the GP to send Darryl into the local hospital for an ECG (a heart tracing) in case an abnormal heartbeat had developed. Darryl was seen by the paediatric registrar, who undertook the ECG, which he felt was normal and discharged Darryl home with advice to return if he worsened.

Darryl's gastroenteritis did not improve, so his mother asked for another GP visit. This second GP called at the home, where he found that Darryl was dehydrated. He recommended clear fluids and arranged to return that afternoon. At this visit he noted that Darryl was worse, so referred him up to the local hospital again. Examination revealed that Darryl was still dehydrated and that he had a very irregular heartbeat. The cardiac centre was contacted and they advised cardioversion (electrical shock to put the heart back to a normal rhythm) followed by immediate transfer to the cardiac centre. The local paediatrician did not feel experienced enough to undertake cardioversion, so arranged urgent transfer. However, just before Darryl was moved to the ambulance he suffered a cardiac arrest and could not be resuscitated. Post mortem showed a blood clot that had obstructed the artery to the lungs.

The claimants argued that Darryl should have been properly assessed, and either kept in the local hospital or referred to the cardiac centre the first time that he was referred by the GP. If that had happened, Darryl's condition could have been monitored, he would not have become dehydrated, and the fatal blood clot would not have formed.

The defendants claimed that the paediatric registrar who undertook the ECG had properly assessed Darryl and that Darryl became dehydrated because his mother had failed to heed medical advice to keep him drinking or to return to the hospital if he got worse.

Review of the first ECG demonstrated that Darryl was suffering from atrial fibrillation (rapid ineffective contraction of the collecting chambers of the heart) which the paediatric registrar had failed to diagnose, this despite the letter from the GP which clearly stated that Darryl's heart rate was irregular and that the cardiac unit had recommended an ECG specifically to rule out atrial fibrillation. The combination of Darryl's underlying complex heart problem and atrial fibrillation produced a situation where clot formation in the heart was significantly increased. The correct method of treating Darryl, therefore, would have been to have diagnosed atrial fibrillation on the first ECG and commenced him on anticoagulants. This would have reduced the chances of clot formation in the heart.

The defendants admitted that atrial fibrillation had been misdiagnosed on the first ECG, but argued that this was a very rare complication of a complicated heart defect. It was not unreasonable, therefore, that the paediatric registrar and consultant were unaware either of this complication or of the need for anticoagulants if atrial fibrillation supervened.

The claimants accepted that it was reasonable that neither doctor was aware of this unusual complication and its subsequent treatment. However, if they were not familiar with the complications of complex heart lesions and the effect of their corrective operations, then there should have been immediate consultation with the heart centre, as indeed the GP had done.

The judge found for the claimants, accepting the argument that a general paediatrician faced with an unknown patient with a complex problem did not have to know the exquisite details of that problem, but should recognise his own limitations and seek assistance from the specialist cardiologists. The judge held that the defendants had been negligent in not diagnosing atrial fibrillation. He also held that the causative link had been established in that the omission of anticoagulants increased the likelihood of clot formation in the heart.

CHAPTER 12

THE RESPIRATORY SYSTEM

INTRODUCTION

The respiratory system consists of all the anatomical aspects necessary to move air from the outside of the body, right down into the lungs to the small air sacs, called alveoli. It is, therefore, quite extensive, so certain parts of the respiratory system can be infected or affected whilst leaving other parts untouched.

ANATOMY

The respiratory system traditionally starts with the external nose, the beginning of the nostrils: nares. Air then moves through the nose and out of the posterior nares into a tube, the nasopharynx. This is blind ending at the top, but in younger children, that is, less than seven years of age, it contains lymph tissue, called adenoids, at the top. Lymph tissue is important in combating infection, but it can also become infected itself. The adenoids may then enlarge, blocking the back of the nose, causing the child to breathe through its mouth and to snore at night. The air then passes down behind the tongue and into the windpipe, or trachea, which is protected from food and drink by a leaf shaped flap at the top, called the epiglottis. The epiglottis moves to protect the trachea during swallowing, and deflects food into the food pipe that lies behind the windpipe, or trachea.

The narrowest part of the trachea is the vocal cords, or voicebox. This is seen externally as the Adam's apple, much more prominent in males than in females. The vocal cords also act as a protection against solid matter entering the lungs. If fluid or solid matter is inhaled past the epiglottis, then the cords will go into spasm, shutting off the rest of the lungs to prevent the fluid or food entering the lungs further down. The foreign material is then expelled out of the trachea by violent coughing.

The windpipe then divides into the right and left main bronchi, which then subdivide into smaller and smaller air passages that end in the small air sacs, the alveoli, where the exchange of oxygen and carbon dioxide happens.

The breathing cycle includes both an active and a passive phase. The active phase is the contraction of the diaphragm, which is dome shaped when relaxed but when it contracts it becomes taut, creating a negative pressure within the chest, so drawing air into the air sacs. At the end of the period of breathing in, or inspiration, there is then immediately expiration, or breathing out. This is essentially passive, and is achieved by the relaxation of the diaphragm and the collapse down of the ribs. After expiration there is a pause before inspiration. The respiratory cycle is therefore inspiration, expiration, pause.

FOREIGN BODIES

Despite the natural defence mechanisms in the respiratory system to stop foreign bodies entering the lungs, this still can happen. Indeed, we have all choked following a drink or some food which has 'gone down the wrong way'. Young children seem particularly prone to inhaling foreign bodies, which is why many toys which include small pieces are not recommended for children less than 36 months of age, and indeed giving peanuts to young children is not recommended. The ability to inhale even quite large objects is also the reason why the tops of Bic biros are now open. The habit of sucking on the end of a biro, dislodging and then inhaling the top, has led to this change, whereby even if the top is impacted in the airways, breathing can continue, albeit through a small orifice.

Foreign bodies, such as pieces of paper or small rubbers, can also be pushed into the nostrils by young children. Eventually, this normally causes a foul smelling discharge from one nostril only. This, however, may not always be the case.

Case study: occult foreign body causing social exclusion

Jodie, aged six, was brought to the Paediatric Outpatients in great distress by her parents. Over the past few months they had noticed that Jodie carried a foul smell around with her. This was despite regular washing of her hair and bathing. The bathing would get rid of the smell for a short period of time, but the smell would return during the day. This had led to Jodie being bullied at school and being shunned by her classmates, which was causing Jodie great distress and she was beginning to refuse to go to school.

Jodie's parents had tried everything they could think of to get rid of the smell and were at their wits' end in that nothing seemed to be successful.

The beginning of the aroma was really quite vague and the parents could remember nothing specific about either when it had occurred or whether there was anything involved in producing this aroma. They had changed Jodie's diet, they had changed her clothes and they had tried to disguise the smell with Eau de Cologne and perfume, all to no avail.

Examination revealed an entirely healthy, bright six year old. Her nose and mouth were clean. There was no suggestion of halitosis (bad breath) and her chest was clear. However, there was a foul and pungent aroma which appeared to be present all over Jodie, and could certainly be smelled all over her head. A tentative diagnosis of inborn error of metabolism was made. This is one of many conditions whereby foodstuffs are not entirely broken down and the unusual waste products are excreted via the skin, leading to odd aromas. This would appear to explain why the smell abated after bathing.

It was agreed that Jodie should come in for some tests to determine whether this was the correct diagnosis, and a further outpatient appointment was made some three weeks later to go through the results.

Jodie and her parents arrived for the follow-up outpatient appointment much relieved. A few days before the appointment, Jodie had started coughing and then sneezed violently, and this had expelled a strip of material that looked like part of a bath sponge. The sponge smelled foul and had the same aroma that Jodie had been emitting for the past few months and, once out, Jodie's own smell became normal. Despite close and sympathetic questioning by the parents, Jodie adamantly denied introducing the sponge into her nostril.

Despite being greatly relieved that Jodie's aroma was now gone, and that the cause of this aroma had become obvious, Jodie's parents were angry that the diagnosis had not been made at the first outpatient appointment. Expert opinion for them concluded that it was inappropriate to make a diagnosis of an inborn error of metabolism when the aroma had not been present either since birth or since starting a mixed solid diet. However, there was only three weeks between the two outpatient appointments so a small *ex gratia* payment was made to Jodie's parents on the basis of Jodie's continued distress at school for those three weeks, during which she had been bullied and shunned by her friends.

RESPIRATORY INFECTIONS

We all suffer at some point from respiratory infections, be it the common cold or upper respiratory tract infection, flu or pneumonia. These infections may be caused either by bacteria or viruses.

Pneumonia

Bacterial

Staphylococcal pneumonia

Staphylococcal pneumonia normally affects young infants, often less than a year of age. It is a devastating and frequently fatal form of pneumonia, during which the lung tissue is destroyed by the *Staphylococcus*. Large abscesses form in the lungs, which, if the child survives, become large useless holes within the lungs. Fortunately, this is now quite an unusual form of pneumonia but should be considered in younger infants who are very unwell and have problems associated with their chests, such as fast breathing or coughing.

Pneumococcal pneumonia

Pneumococcal pneumonia, caused by *Streptococcus pneumoniae*, is one of the commoner forms of bacterial pneumonia in healthy children. It tends to affect children in the first decade of life, but can affect any age group. The lungs are divided up on each side into sections, called lobes, and within those, lobules. Classically, pneumococcal pneumonia infects the whole of one lobe or lobule, and therefore is seen on chest x-ray as a sharp edged white area against the black of normal air. This is so typical of pneumococcal pneumonia that no further investigations need to be undertaken and the child can be treated with penicillin. However, there are now increasing reports of penicillin-resistant *Pneumococcus*, so recommendations now are to use two antibiotics, such as penicillin and an antibiotic called azithromycin.

A child with pneumococcal pneumonia is often quite unwell. They have rapid breathing and the cycle of respiration may be altered, so that inspiration is followed by a pause and then expiration, followed immediately by inspiration, reversal of the respiratory cycle. If the pneumonia is extensive, then the child's lips and tongue may be deep red instead of pink, or even blue, indicating that the child is having difficulty in getting enough oxygen into the blood stream.

Listening to a child's chest is of vital importance. However, because the chest is small in young children, it may be possible to hear air moving in and out of the chest normally on both sides despite the child having pneumonia, because sounds are transmitted from one side of the chest to the other. If there is any doubt, a chest x-ray is therefore mandatory. This type of confusion can occur in any form of pneumonia.

Failure to diagnose pneumonia can lead to local or even distant problems. The pneumonia may develop into an abscess, and the abscess may rupture through the lung causing pus to lie between the outside surface of the lung and the inside surface of the rib cage. This pus does not usually respond to antibiotics, as it is difficult to get a high enough concentration of antibiotic into pus. It will either have to be drained by passing a tube into the chest or, on occasions, may actually need surgical removal. Abscess formation within the lungs may also rupture into the blood vessels, and if that happens then the infection can be carried around the body, causing multiple sites of infection and abscesses around the body. Prompt diagnosis and effective treatment is therefore important in trying to reduce the frequency of these local or distant complications. However, these complications can occur even with prompt utilisation of antibiotics, or may have occurred before the child presents to a doctor. The presence of complications, therefore, does not necessarily connote negligence.

Atypical pneumonia

There are other organisms that are either bacterial or bacteria-like which can also cause pneumonia in children. The child often presents in a similar way with a cough, being unwell and rapid breathing. However, chest x-ray will reveal a different, more scattered, pattern of shadows on the lungs. Both lungs may also be infected. In this case, it is important to use two antibiotics together, such as amoxycillin and azithromycin, to cover these unusual bacteria.

Tuberculosis

Tuberculosis still exists in our society and can affect all ages. The commonest form of tuberculosis in children is tuberculous pneumonia. Certain racial groups are more at risk of developing tuberculosis as children. These include children of Asian parentage, and there is now a national programme for immunisation with BCG of all children of Asian origin before discharge from hospital following birth. The inoculation, which is given intradermally (into the skin layer), is given on the upper left arm. This should cause scarring and so it is easy to see whether a child has been inoculated or not. It is important to remember, however, that BCG inoculation, although reducing the chances of developing tuberculosis, does not guarantee completely that the child will not develop tuberculosis if exposed to the organism.

Children from races which are not considered at high risk receive BCG immunisation at around 13 years of life. Before that time, therefore, they are theoretically vulnerable to developing tuberculosis. Frank chest tuberculosis is unusual in children, so the commonest reason for children to be treated is following their contact with an adult in their near or extended family who has developed open chest tuberculosis. However, the diagnosis of tuberculosis must be kept in mind in children who fail to respond to antibiotics that would be expected to cure a bacterial infection, or in children who have an unusual chest x-ray. The diagnosis must be entertained in all children who fulfil these criteria, regardless of their racial origin.

There are two broad categories of TB in children. As this is their first exposure to tuberculosis, they have primary tuberculosis. This can be localised, with an area of pneumonia often in the upper part of the lung, with enlarged glands in the centre of the chest. The other form is so called miliary TB. In this form the tuberculosis extends throughout both lungs, with very fine 'millet seed' sized white patches throughout the lung. Another way of describing it is a 'snow storm lung'.

Children respond well to anti-tuberculous treatment. The antibiotics used for tuberculosis are completely different from those used for any other form of pneumonia, and are also used for several weeks. Without treatment, however, tuberculosis is fatal and miliary tuberculosis, the form in which the pneumonia is throughout both lungs, can be relatively rapidly fatal.

Case study: missed diagnosis of tuberculosis causing avoidable death

Eli, aged three, had had a cough for several weeks. His mother had taken him down to the general practitioner, who had treated him with a course of amoxycillin for a week. This had produced no improvement in Eli's cough, indeed if anything it was slightly worse. The GP then prescribed a course of erythromycin, again for a week. Again there was no improvement, so the GP thought that Eli probably had a viral chest infection, which was why it was not responding to antibiotics. However, two weeks later, Eli's mother took him back to the GP. She felt that Eli was not particularly well, he wasn't eating well and he was still coughing. The GP then gave Eli a 10-day course of cefuroxime. Eli's mother religiously gave him the antibiotics, but after 10 days there was no improvement. She waited a further week before taking him back to the GP.

The GP had examined Eli's chest on each occasion and felt there was nothing abnormal, but on the last examination he wondered if there were a few crepitations (crackly sounds in the chest) and referred him to the local hospital.

The history of multiple antibiotics with no improvement in Eli's condition was noted. It was felt that he was breathing rather rapidly, and a chest x-ray revealed small scattered white shadows throughout both lung fields. It was felt that Eli had atypical pneumonia, despite the fact that he had not responded to erythromycin, which is an appropriate antibiotic for such pneumonia. He was treated with a different antibiotic appropriate for atypical pneumonia. However, over the next 48 hours Eli deteriorated. He now required oxygen to maintain adequate oxygen levels in his blood and he was refusing to eat at all.

A repeat chest x-ray was ordered which showed worsening of the scattered shadows throughout his chest, and it was felt that he might have an unusual form of atypical pneumonia, one which normally affects children who have an abnormality with their immune system. He was therefore treated with high-dose antibiotics appropriate for this unusual atypical pneumonia and his immune system tested. The results of this were normal.

Over the next few days, Eli deteriorated further. Miliary TB was considered and he was tested for TB infection with a Mantoux test in his forearm. This remained negative. As Eli deteriorated further, requiring more oxygen, he was commenced on further drugs for an unusual pneumonia, *Cytomegalovirus* pneumonia. Despite this intensive regimen of multiple antibiotics, Eli continued to deteriorate, and 10 days after admission he suffered a respiratory and cardiac arrest from which he could not be resuscitated.

Post mortem revealed a pneumonia consistent with miliary tuberculosis, and the tubercle bacillus was grown from Eli's sputum sent ante mortem.

His mother claimed that a diagnosis of tuberculosis should have been considered in Eli as he had not responded to three courses of different antibiotics by the GP and deteriorated despite antibiotics in hospital. Although he was a white Caucasian, the first chest x-ray taken on admission was suspicious of miliary TB and the second x-ray, taken two days later, eight days before he died, was considered classical of miliary TB. The expert witness concluded, however, that it was reasonable to treat Eli for atypical pneumonia as the initial diagnosis. However, it was inappropriate to consider as the next most likely diagnosis pneumocystis carinii pneumonia, which is normally only seen in children with severe immune problems. Eli had been previously entirely healthy, there were no risk factors for any abnormality with his immune system, and although the chest x-ray was consistent with pneumocystis carinii pneumonia, it was also consistent with tuberculosis, which was a much more likely diagnosis in a previously healthy child.

The negative Mantoux test for tuberculosis should not have been considered a contraindication to treatment as it is well recognised that during miliary TB, the Mantoux test is frequently negative. The expert witness for liability concluded that Eli should have been started on anti-tuberculous therapy following the second x-ray eight days before he died. The causation expert witness provided compelling evidence that, had antituberculous therapy been started at that point, Eli would have made a complete recovery, thus liability and causation were proven. The case was not contested.

Bronchopneumonia

There are two main types of bronchopneumonia: viral and aspiration bronchopneumonia. Viral bronchopneumonia occurs in otherwise healthy children. Aspiration bronchopneumonia normally occurs in children with learning and mobility difficulties who have inco-ordination of chewing, breathing and swallowing, such as in cerebral palsy, so they may then inhale foodstuff into their airways.

Viral bronchopneumonia

Any infection in the alveoli or air sacs in children reduces the capacity to exchange oxygen and carbon dioxide. This is more of a problem in younger children, in that the number of air sacs they possess is considerably less than the adult number (the adult number of air sacs is normally achieved between the ages of 8 and 10 years). If there is compromise to oxygen and carbon dioxide exchange, then the body's natural reaction is to increase the rate of breathing. This allows carbon dioxide to be removed, but it is less effective at increasing oxygen in the blood. Thus, even in viral pneumonia, which is usually a mild illness, the child may present with some difficulty in breathing.

Examination of the chest may again reveal nothing abnormal, so chest x-ray is important. The chest x-ray in viral bronchopneumonia shows patchy small shadows affecting only small parts of the lungs, but possibly scattered throughout the lung fields. Although bronchopneumonia is viral in origin, sometimes the atypical pneumonias can show a similar chest x-ray and so many units will tend to treat children in whom the clinical diagnosis is viral bronchopneumonia with antibiotics, just to make sure that an atypical pneumonia is not missed. In this case, treatment is normally with one or two antibiotics designed to cover the atypical pneumonia.

Aspiration bronchopneumonia

This occurs when food particles are inhaled into the lungs. This may be during chewing and swallowing if there is considerable inco-ordination of eating. There may well be choking as the vocal cords go into spasm to try to protect the lung, but even so, food particles may drop into the lungs. Because of the anatomy of the lungs, food and liquid tends to pass into the right lung. Another way of aspirating is for food to wash up into the gullet and then tip over from the gullet into the trachea. This is gastro-oesophageal reflux. This may occur, for example, in children with significant physical difficulties who may not be able to sit up and may be lying almost in the supine position. Once foodstuff gets into the lungs, it causes inflammation in the air sacs and predisposes the child to a bacterial infection in the areas of damage, and this can lead on to small abscess formation. If aspiration pneumonia is suspected or diagnosed, antibiotic therapy may be appropriate.

Aspiration pneumonia is a major factor in determining life expectancy in children and adults with motor abnormalities, such as cerebral palsy.

CYSTIC FIBROSIS

Cystic fibrosis is the commonest inherited chest problem in Western Europe. It occurs in approximately one in every 2,000 births and is inherited by the so called autosomal recessive route. That means that the parents are unaffected, but each possesses a normal gene and a 'cystic fibrosis' gene. If the two cystic fibrosis genes come together then that particular child suffers from the disease. The chance of this happening in any such couple is one in four for each pregnancy.

The major problem with cystic fibrosis is an abnormality in the way secretions are made, and they become very sticky. This affects the secretions in the lungs, but eventually cystic fibrosis will cause damage to other organs such as the pancreas and the liver. Its effects, therefore, are not restricted to the lungs, although it is frequently the lung problems that are the most problematic.

The lungs produce mucus constantly and this is moved by little hairs, called cilia, up and away from the alveoli, or air sacs, through the lungs and eventually out of the trachea into the gullet, and the mucus is swallowed. This movement of mucus hardly happens in cystic fibrosis and because of this, there is a highly increased chance of chest infections. Indeed, a common way that cystic fibrosis may be diagnosed is following repeated chest infections in the first year or few years of life.

There is presently no cure for cystic fibrosis, and treatment consists of aggressive antibiotic therapy for chest infections and maintenance of adequate nutrition.

The secretions into the gut are also very viscid (an older name for cystic fibrosis was mucoviscidosis), and sometimes this causes problems with the passage of stool, especially the infant stool, called meconium. One of the differential diagnoses of delayed passage of meconium is cystic fibrosis. At term, 96% of all infants pass meconium within the first 24 hours and 98.5% within the first 48 hours. Cystic fibrosis is not the only cause for delayed passage of meconium, but it should certainly be considered as a possibility in a term infant who has demonstrated such a problem.

This rule cannot be applied to pre-term babies, as the gut is not mature and does not function properly and so delayed passage of first stool is very common.

Case study: appropriate investigation for delayed passage of meconium

Holly was the fifth child of unrelated parents. Her mother smoked 15–20 cigarettes daily, but the pregnancy was otherwise uncomplicated and Holly's mother went into spontaneous labour at 40 weeks plus three days. The birth was uncomplicated, Holly needed no resuscitation and her birth weight was 3.2 kg. She fed well and returned to the postnatal ward with her mother.

The paediatricians were called on the second day of life when Holly had not passed meconium. Holly had been feeding well, had not vomited and was very settled. Examination revealed a modestly distended abdomen, normal bowel sounds and a patent anus. Rectal examination was unremarkable and following the extraction of the finger, meconium was passed. A diagnosis of a meconium plug was made and Holly's mother was reassured. Holly then presented at the age of four months and at seven months with pneumonia. It was noted on her second admission that her weight gain had been poor and a sweat test confirmed a diagnosis of cystic fibrosis. Her chest infection was treated aggressively with antibiotics and she made an excellent recovery. She was started on enzyme supplements, given a high calorie diet, and thereafter gained weight satisfactorily.

The claimants argued that Holly should have been investigated for cystic fibrosis as part of the differential diagnosis of delayed passage of meconium. Had she been tested, the diagnosis would have been made earlier, Holly would have been treated appropriately, would have gained weight adequately and was less likely to have suffered two chest infections in the first year of life. Had there been any chest signs, Holly would have been treated early and aggressively with antibiotics. As she had had two chest infections in the first year of life, this meant that there had already been lung damage and this worsened her prognosis for normal lung function thereafter.

The defendants argued that cystic fibrosis was only one of several possible diagnoses for failure of passage of meconium. It would be inappropriate to test the 4% of all term infants who did not pass meconium on the first day of life and that, as meconium had been passed following rectal examination, the diagnosis of meconium plug was not unreasonable. The defendants further argued that, even if causation was accepted, the randomised trial of screening for cystic fibrosis at birth versus making a diagnosis on clinical grounds, undertaken in the West Midlands in the 1980s and 1990s, clearly came to the conclusion that by the age of two years there was no difference in clinical state between children who had been diagnosed at birth and those that had been diagnosed within the first year of life. Thus, no long term harm had come to Holly courtesy of the delay of seven months to diagnosis.

Following advice from Counsel, the case did not proceed.

ASTHMA

Asthma is a member of the atopic (allergic) family of asthma, eczema and hay fever. Commonly in children with asthma there is a family history of a parent or close relative with one or more of those illnesses. Asthma has a genetic basis in that the child is born with the propensity to develop asthma, and whether the child actually does develop asthma depends on environmental factors and triggers. Asthma can occur at any age after the age of one year, but there is still controversy as to whether asthma does occur in children under one year of age. However, there does seem to be consensus that asthma is difficult to diagnose in infants less than six months of age.

Asthma is characterised by wheezing and difficulty in moving air in and out of the lungs. Normally it is more difficult to breathe out during an asthma attack than breathe in. This is because when a negative pressure is produced by the contraction of the diaphragm, the airways open up a little bit, allowing air to pass in. When the diaphragm relaxes and the rib cage collapses, the diameter of the airways reduces, making it difficult to shift air out. Young children with asthma may not have a wheeze, they may just have a cough, which connotes an exacerbation of asthma.

There are many triggers which can cause an exacerbation of asthma; these include excitement, house dust mite, animal dander, pollen and also such things as mould spores and smoking. These factors, however, trigger an attack of asthma. None of them will cause the child to have asthma in the first place: that is determined by the genetic predisposition of the child.

There is no cure for asthma, although happily many children do grow out of it in their teenage years. Treatment is therefore directed at trying to prevent an attack of asthma or by relieving the attack of asthma. Attempts at preventing an asthma attack include avoidance of known trigger factors if possible, but also the use of regular inhaled steroids, which are effective in preventing attacks of asthma, although not completely. If a child does develop asthma or wheeze, then they are treated with an asthma reliever which opens up the airways, improving the child's ability to move air in and out.

Housing conditions

House dust mite

The environment in which children spend much of their life, that is, their home, can have a profound effect on the control of asthma in predisposed children. The house dust mite is ubiquitous, except in brand new houses, and it lives on human skin scales. With the advent of fitted carpets, the load of house dust mites in any house with such carpets has increased considerably. Allergy to house dust mite is a well recognised trigger for asthma. In severe cases it may be appropriate to remove carpeting and use lino on the floor, and to wet dusters or mops to prevent clouds of house dust mites billowing into the air. This is only appropriate in children who react severely to house dust mite, as the effort expended in marginally reducing the load of house dust mite in a house is not commensurate with the improvement in asthma in children at the mild to moderate end of the spectrum.

Smoking

Secondary, or passive, smoking can also exacerbate asthma and it is well recognised that children who live in a smoky atmosphere are at risk from asthma exacerbations. Smoke particles are ubiquitous in houses where smoking occurs, so it is not helpful if one room in the house is designated the 'smoking room'. The other rooms within the house will also become contaminated by smoke particles. Smoking only outside is similarly unhelpful, as smoke particles are introduced into the house on clothing.

Damp and mould

Mould spores are associated with acute exacerbations of asthma. Most houses will have some mould, especially around the windows in kitchens and bathrooms, which are generally quite damp. However, houses that are generally damp, either from rising damp or penetrating damp with superadded mould infestation, can have a deleterious effect on a child's asthma. This can be quite dramatic, with children suffering either mild or infrequent attacks of asthma in one house and then suffering quite severe and frequent attacks when they move into a damp and mouldy house. The asthma can abate if the root cause of the damp and mould is removed or, again, if the family moves on to a dry house.

Temperature within the house itself is not important. It matters not whether there is central heating or individual gas or electric fires. The temperature difference is important, however, in that children may develop asthma if they go from a warm atmosphere, such as a centrally heated house, out into the cold fresh air. Interestingly, there is no evidence that hot air central heating, which must stir up clouds of dust, is associated with exacerbation of asthma.

Case study: exacerbation of asthma following exposure to damp and mould

Geoffrey and his family moved council houses when he was four years of age. He had previously been diagnosed as having asthma by his GP and had been referred to the local hospital Outpatients. He was treated for his asthma with regular low-dose inhaled steroids and the occasional use of salbutamol, an asthma reliever.

The house that the family moved into was in poor condition but was larger, which was the reason for moving given the increasing size of Geoffrey's family. There was inadequate ventilation in the bathroom and in the kitchen and there was penetrating damp in the bedroom that Geoffrey and his two brothers used and in the downstairs living room. There was a considerable amount of mould on the external wall in Geoffrey's bedroom, on the ceilings in the kitchen and the bathroom, and on the damp wall in the living room. Shortly after moving, Geoffrey was admitted for the first time with an acute exacerbation of asthma. He had frequent attacks of asthma, which necessitated an increase in inhaled steroid dosage, and also an increased use of his asthma reliever.

The council recognised that repair works needed to be done and had promised this to the family when they moved in. However, it took some four years for all the repairs to be effected, after which the house was dry and mould-free. There was a significant improvement in Geoffrey's asthma following repairs.

Geoffrey's parents claimed that the conditions within the house had worsened Geoffrey's asthma and that he had suffered four years of unnecessarily severe asthma, as the Council had failed to carry out the repairs as speedily as the family had been promised on moving into the house. The defendants pointed out that both parents smoked and that smoking was a much more potent trigger for asthma attacks than mould spores. Thus, the majority of problems suffered by Geoffrey with regards to his asthma related to parental smoking.

The claimants countered that they had always smoked and they were continuing to smoke, but that Geoffrey's asthma had worsened when moving into the present house and had improved when the repairs had been finished. Thus, although smoking might be a trigger to asthma attacks, that had been a constant feature and so the worsening and subsequent improvement within the house must have related entirely to the mould and damp within the house. A settlement was agreed out of court.

Pets

Much is made of the effect of pets on childhood asthma. There are certainly some children who have an attack of asthma if they are in contact with certain animals. Long-haired dogs and cats tend to be more of a problem in homes than their short-haired counterparts. Skin testing children may produce a positive reaction to certain animals, but it is important to be sure that the animal in question does actually cause asthma before getting rid of it. Many children who have asthma can perfectly happily cope with dogs and cats and other furry pets at home. It is also worth remembering that even if the animal is banished from the house, the hairs from that animal, if it has been around for some time, will take a considerable period of time, many months, to disappear, despite regular vacuum cleaning. Thus the banishment of an animal will not result in an immediate improvement in the asthma of the child.

CHAPTER 13

THE ABDOMINAL SYSTEM

INTRODUCTION

The abdominal system includes the gastrointestinal tract, which is basically the gut from mouth to anus, as well as the organs situated in the abdominal cavity itself. These include the kidney, liver, spleen and internal genitalia, of which the female genitalia is of greater importance. Traditionally the gastrointestinal tract has been separated into upper and lower parts.

UPPER GASTROINTESTINAL TRACT

This encompasses the mouth, oesophagus (gullet or food pipe), stomach and small intestines.

Mouth

Saliva is produced in, and food and drink taken into, the mouth. These substances must then be swallowed in a co-ordinated way. The food and fluids are forced to the back of the mouth by the tongue and during swallowing the soft palate closes off the back of the nose to prevent food and fluid being forced out through the nose. The epiglottis, the leaf like flap protecting the trachea (breathing tube) also closes off, so the bolus of fluid or food passes down into the oesophagus (gullet) without compromising breathing. Once in the gullet, waves of pressure propel the food and fluid down into the stomach.

Oesophagus

The gullet is an active organ. It does not function like a drainpipe, with food and fluid just dropping into the stomach; they are actively propelled.

Inco-ordination of swallowing and breathing potentially leads to fluid or foodstuff entering the lungs. This can cause aspiration pneumonia and is also a factor in determining life expectancy in children who have neurological problems affecting co-ordination of swallowing, as may occur in cerebral palsy.

Food and fluid can enter the mouth, but so also can foreign bodies. This is especially important in young infants, who go through an 'oral' phase of development beginning around eight or nine months of age. During this time, infants are very inquisitive and use their mouth as part of experiencing new objects. All sorts of things, therefore, are put in the mouth as part of normal development. Some of these may be swallowed. If large, they can cause choking and may get stuck either in the back of the throat or in the gullet. They may be sharp, such as pins or safety pins, or they may be small and run the risk of entering the lungs.

The gullet is the narrowest part of the gut, so normally if a foreign body can pass through the gullet and enter the stomach, it is safe to allow the child to pass the foreign body with stool, unless it is poisonous, such as mercury batteries.

Case study: food refusal as a clue to a foreign body stuck in the gullet

Alexander was taken to the GP when he was 16 months. Until that point, he had been developing normally and had been eating and drinking adequately. He was thriving and gaining weight. Both his parents worked full time and he was cared for at home by a full time nanny. Alexander had suddenly stopped taking solid food, although he would drink. This had occurred following two days during which he had taken solid food, but then regurgitated it, undigested, almost immediately. Thereafter, he refused to take solids at all.

His mother had tried to coax him by offering him his favourite foods, but this had not worked. He was examined by the GP, who found nothing abnormal at all and reassured his mother that Alexander would forget about this episode and would start eating normally. However, two weeks later Alexander was beginning to lose weight, although his mother had ingeniously devised ways of maintaining calorie intake in liquid form. He was taken back to his GP, who then referred him on to the local general paediatrician. The paediatrician found a similar history, again examined Alexander, took a detailed developmental history that was entirely normal, and again reassured his mother and the nanny that there was nothing wrong with Alexander.

However, a further outpatient appointment in a month's time was made in case Alexander had not started eating.

Indeed, it transpired that this was the case. Alexander would become very distressed when offered solid food but would drink any type of fluid with enthusiasm. Again Alexander was examined carefully, but nothing abnormal was found.

His mother demanded a chest x-ray just in case there was something wrong in Alexander's chest. The paediatrician was disinclined so to do, but eventually acceded to Alexander's mother's wishes. Chest x-ray revealed a coin lodged between the upper third and the lower two thirds of Alexander's oesophagus. This was removed at operation, but it took another six weeks of slow coaxing and offering very small amounts of solid food before Alexander was eating normally again.

The claimants felt that the diagnosis should have been made on the first visit to the paediatrician. He should have ordered a chest x-ray, as Alexander had already been looked after by his GP and no improvement had occurred. The claimants demanded compensation for a month's extra discomfort. The defendants' expert witness felt that the paediatrician had been negligent in that specific questions concerning foreign bodies had not been asked. The Trust's solicitors indicated that the amount of money involved was so small that it was not worth considering further defence and settlement was made.

Stomach

Once food and fluid is in the stomach it is normally discharged into the intestines. However, many babies suffer from gastro-oesophageal reflux. This is when the contents of the stomach wash back up into the lower part of the gullet. Occasionally this can be so severe that food stuff actually washes back up the entire length of the gullet and may spill over into the lungs, causing aspiration pneumonia. The contents of the stomach are very acid, and the lining of the oesophagus is not designed to withstand acid. Chronic gastro-oesophageal reflux can therefore lead to inflammation of the gullet. This can eventually cause erosion of the lining of the gullet and, on occasions, scar tissue may form, causing narrowing of the lower part of the gullet. This, however, only occurs after long term gastro-oesophageal reflux.

Small intestine

Food is partially digested in the stomach, turned into semi-liquid form and then discharged into the intestines. Here the acidity of the stomach contents is neutralised by secretions from the pancreas. Continuing digestion and absorption of foodstuff occurs in the small intestine before the intestinal contents arrive at the junction between the small intestine and the large intestine.

LOWER GASTROINTESTINAL TRACT

Large intestine

The main role of the large intestine is to extract fluid from the intestinal contents, which is why we pass formed, soft but solid, stools.

The time taken for food to pass from the mouth, through the intestines and out through the anus varies enormously between individuals. However, for the majority of the population a passage time of one to three days would be considered normal.

ABDOMINAL ORGANS

Liver

The liver's main roles are to act as a food store and to digest waste products from the body, which are discharged via bile back into the intestine. It is the colour of the bile that determines the colour of the eventual stool. If there is a blockage to the flow of bile, for example, stools are very light in colour, almost white.

The liver is important in metabolising many drugs and antibiotics. It is also important in getting rid of alcohol from the bloodstream and so is a highly complex organ. Because of these complexities, liver failure can only be treated by liver transplant. There is no equivalent of renal dialysis in the case of liver failure. Fortunately, there is much spare capacity in the liver so that physical damage to the liver, such as in trauma or loss of liver bulk for tumours, does not necessarily lead to inadequate liver function.

Spleen

The spleen, which is on the left side of the abdomen, is involved in fighting infection and also in destruction of red blood cells. Red blood cells last, on average, around 120 days, and at the end of this time they are destroyed in the spleen. The iron from red blood cells is recycled, but the remnants of the cells are passed to the liver, which converts them into bile, which is then discharged into the gut. The spleen is very important, especially in children, when it comes to fighting certain types of infection. The loss of the spleen in itself is not fatal. We can all function without a spleen. However, children especially are much more prone to particular infections when they lose the spleen. They then need to be vaccinated against an organism called *Pneumococcus* and to take prophylactic penicillin on a daily basis.

The spleen can be ruptured by trauma, such as in a car accident, or by blunt trauma to the abdomen, such as stamping. If this is not diagnosed, because the spleen has such a good blood supply children can die by internal haemorrhaging into the abdomen (see case study, Chapter 9, p 75).

Pancreas

The pancreas is also a highly complicated organ. It produces many enzymes which help digest the foodstuff in the gut, and it also produces fluid to counteract the acidity of the stomach. It is also important in controlling sugar levels in the body by producing hormones. Insulin lowers the level of sugar in the body and glucagon raises the level of sugar in the body. These two enzymes are important, therefore, in maintaining control over blood sugar levels, although many other hormones are also important.

The pancreas is set deep in the abdomen and is very rarely damaged by trauma. It may cause abdominal pain if it is infected, especially by the mumps virus, but the commonest cause of damage in children is secondary to cystic fibrosis, which causes excess stickiness of the fluid from the pancreas to the gut. This build-up eventually causes destruction of the pancreas. Children with cystic fibrosis, therefore, need to take extra pancreatic enzymes by mouth and may eventually develop diabetes.

Kidneys

The kidney's main function is to filter the blood, extracting waste products which are then passed in the urine. Protein is vital for growth and maintenance of the body, but we do not utilise all parts of protein molecules, which if left in the body can become toxic. The main route of elimination of these protein bi-products is in the urine.

Some drugs are excreted in the urine, so it is the urine that is analysed in cases where children are thought possibly to have taken drugs, either as part of an intentional overdose or recreational drugs.

The kidneys produce hormones which are important in controlling blood pressure (renin), and which also control bone marrow function to maintain the level of red blood cells circulating in the body (erythropoietin).

The urinary tract that encompasses the kidneys, ureters (the tube connecting the kidneys to the bladder), and the urethra (tube to the outside) is open to the outside. Thus there is a potential for urine to be infected. This is particularly common in girls, as the urethra (tube to the outside) opens on to the surface of the body relatively close to the anus. Bacteria can migrate from the anus up the urethra, causing an infection in the urine. This is much less common in boys, for obvious anatomical reasons.

Any abnormality in the urinary tract, such as a congenital narrowing in the ureters (tubes from the kidney to the bladder), or if there is reflux, that is urine moving up towards the kidneys during micturition, increases the chances of children having urinary tract infections.

The combination of infected urine and reflux of this infected urine into the kidneys in young children can cause infection of the kidneys, with eventual loss of part of the kidneys. If this loss becomes substantial, then there is a risk of high blood pressure and also kidney failure as the child gets older. It is vital, therefore, that any child who has a proven infection in the urine is investigated fully.

Urinary tract infection

These investigations vary with the age of the child. Several guidelines as to which investigations are necessary at what ages have been written, but as yet there is no absolute consensus as to how children with a urinary tract infection should be investigated.

The kidneys are only at risk of being infected and scarred when the children are quite young. At this age, normally taken to be below two years of age, any urinary tract infection must be investigated with an ultrasound scan of the kidneys, a radio-isotope scan looking for scarring (DMSA scan), and a micturating cystourethrogram (MCUG). This is specifically to look for reflux of urine up the ureters. In this investigation, a small catheter is introduced through the urethra into the bladder, radio-opaque dye is introduced into the bladder, and x-rays taken while the child is passing urine. With these three investigations it should be possible to determine whether there is any anatomical abnormality with the kidneys, ureters or bladder, or whether there is any reflux. If there is significant reflux, then the child should be put on to a low-dose prophylactic antibiotic to reduce the chances of subsequent urine infections.

Above two, the child should have a renal ultrasound scan and also a DMSA scan, again looking for anatomical abnormalities and scarring. If any abnormalities are found, then further investigations may be warranted.

Above the age of five, the only investigation needed is a renal ultrasound. Further investigations may be indicated depending on the finding of that ultrasound.

Because of the potential severity of outcome of young children having an undetected urinary tract infection which can lead on to to severe renal scarring, all children under the age of one that are admitted into hospital have a routine urine test for infection undertaken.

Case study: inadequate investigation of childhood urinary infections causing later kidney failure

Hilda was referred up by her GP at the age of 13 because she had been complaining of headaches. She had been treated unsuccessfully by her GP with painkillers. Examination at the local hospital revealed that Hilda had very high blood pressure. It was unclear whether this was related to the anxiety of coming to hospital or whether this was Hilda's normal blood pressure.

It was arranged for her to have her blood pressure taken several times in the GP's surgery, where she felt quite relaxed, and each time the blood pressure was greatly elevated.

The high blood pressure was cautiously treated to return the blood pressure to a normal level and Hilda underwent several investigations, after which it was found that she had very small, scarred kidneys.

A more detailed history was then taken, when it became clear that Hilda had been treated for a urinary tract infection when she was three years of age by her GP. There was another episode when she was five years old that clinically may have been a urinary tract infection also.

The abnormal kidney findings were consistent with scarring following infection of the kidneys that would have occurred in the first few years of Hilda's life.

The claimants argued that the GP should have referred Hilda for investigations after her first episode of a urine infection. Had that happened, the extent of any kidney damage would have been elucidated some 10 years earlier and Hilda could have been put onto therapy to reduce the chances of any further infections and continuing kidney damage.

The defendants argued that even if Hilda had been referred at the age of three, on the balance of probabilities, she would already have suffered some degree of renal scarring as this occurs mainly before the age of two. The expert witnesses on both sides agreed that it was likely that some degree of renal damage would have occurred before Hilda's urinary tract infection became obvious, and she would have suffered urinary tract infections which were not obvious to her parents in the first year or so of life. However, they could not agree as to the likely degree of damage compared with the virtual destruction of the kidneys that was present when Hilda was investigated at the local hospital.

The case went to trial, with the claimants suggesting that 80% of the kidney damage had occurred after the age of three, with the defendants arguing exactly the opposite.

The judge agreed that the majority of the kidney damage was likely to have occurred before the age of two years, which he assessed at 60% of the present kidney damage, and thus awarded 40% of damages to the claimants.

Auto-immune renal disease

The kidneys can also suffer damage which is thought to be inflicted by the body's own immune system, so called auto-immune damage. In this case, the body's immune defences are triggered by a stimulus but then confuse the normal kidney tissue for foreign tissue and attack it. This can occur after an infection with a particular organism called *Streptococcus*, for example, a sore throat: post-streptococcal glomerulonephritis. It can also occur as part of a more generalised auto-immune disease where the gut, kidneys and joints may be affected: Henoch–Schoenlein purpura. Fortunately, the outcome in both these diseases is normally very good. In glomerulonephritis, there may be high blood pressure that needs to be treated and there may be a need to reduce fluid intake for a while, but the kidneys normally rapidly recover.

Good recovery is also true in Henoch–Schoenlein purpura. There may be slightly raised blood pressure, and bleeding from the kidneys, and therefore blood in the urine. Treatment is normally directed at the pain from the joint or intestinal involvement. However, occasionally some children do suffer badly from both glomerulonephritis and Henoch–Schoenlein purpura. Treatment of severe kidney involvement in these illnesses is difficult, and not always effective.

Case study: the effect of the timing of referral to specialist renal unit

Susan, aged eight, developed Henoch–Schoenlein purpura (HSP). Her parents noticed a rash, mainly over her legs and buttocks, and took her to her GP, who referred Susan on to the hospital with a diagnosis of HSP. Investigations at the hospital revealed that she had blood in her urine, her blood pressure was normal, but one wrist and one ankle were slightly swollen. She was admitted and the following day she was complaining bitterly of pain in her swollen joints.

Her blood tests showed that her kidney function was normal and that her full blood count was normal. She made a rapid recovery and was discharged three days later. However, the last ward urine test showed that she was still passing a lot of blood in her urine. She was seen in Outpatients, and blood tests were repeated which showed that, although still within normal limits, a marker of kidney function (creatinine) had risen by 50%. She was still passing blood in her urine.

The following month she defaulted from her outpatient appointment but was seen the following month, when she was still passing blood in her urine, her kidney function test (creatinine) had risen further and her blood count had dropped by 1.5 g/dl. A decision was made to see her in three months' time.

At this outpatient appointment she was still passing blood in her urine. Blood tests were taken and she was sent home. The blood tests revealed grossly abnormal kidney function and she was called back urgently and referred on to a specialist paediatric kidney unit. They treated her with drugs which have been shown to have some effect in kidney failure secondary to HSP, but unfortunately her kidney function deteriorated and she had to go on to kidney dialysis. Her kidney function never recovered.

The claimants argued that Susan should have been referred to a specialist kidney unit at the time when her kidney function had shown signs of deterioration. If she had been referred at that time, then she would have been followed by a specialist paediatric renal unit who would have started early drug therapy, thus improving the chances of success. The defendants argued that there was no indication to refer Susan on to a specialist unit at that point. The outcome of most children with HSP is good, and there was no particular cause for concern with regard to Susan. Susan was then referred on to the specialist kidney unit when there was evidence of kidney damage. Further, the drugs with which Susan was treated had a variable effect and as they did not have any positive effect on Susan's kidney function when they were started, then there was no evidence they would have had any positive effect had they been started earlier.

The judge found for the claimants on liability, and stated that Susan should have been referred to the paediatric renal unit at the second outpatient appointment that Susan attended and not merely been given another appointment for three months. However, he found for the defendants on causation, as the published medical evidence did not support the argument that the drugs used on Susan were effective.

GENITALIA

Genitalia are classified as either external, that is, visible, or internal. The female genitalia are the only genitalia of significance within the abdominal cavity.

Testis

The testis develops in the fetus in the same sort of area as the kidney. Towards the end of pregnancy, the testes descend from that area down through the groin and into the scrotum. The blood supply, however, still comes from abdominal vessels. A percentage of testes either do not descend or descend abnormally. It is well recognised that unless the testes are in the scrotum, fertility is reduced, as the testes need to be at a slightly lower temperature than the normal body temperature of 37°C. There is also a problem of cancer developing in undescended testes. Thus, boys whose testes have not descended at birth, and do not descend in the first year of life, undergo an operation, orchidopexy, to locate the testes in the scrotum. Care must be undertaken during operation, as the blood supply to the testes is still from abdominal vessels. If the testes are pulled down too far, the blood supply can be compromised, jeopardising the survival of the testes.

Case study: insufficient care during operative scrotal location causing loss of testes

Harold's birth was met with great delight by his parents and extended family. He was the first son after two daughters, and the first grandson after seven granddaughters. His father checked him over quickly and felt that all his 'bits' were present and correct. However, the paediatrician, examining Harold the next day, noted that neither testis was present in the scrotum. The paediatrician explained that if Harold's testes did not descend of the their own accord, he would have to undergo an operation in the first few years of life to locate the testes in the scrotum.

He was referred to the paediatric surgeons, who merely observed Harold's progress, but as descent did not occur, they elected to undertake surgery at the age of three years. The testes were located quite high in the abdomen but were brought down into the scrotum and stitched in place in one operation.

Harold's father became somewhat concerned when Harold was 14 years old that he was showing no signs of sexual maturation. His GP examined Harold and could find no evidence of testicular tissue in the scrotum, and referred him on to a paediatric endocrinologist.

No testicular tissue could be found and hormonal investigations indicated that Harold could not produce testosterone, indicating that there was no viable testicular tissue. Harold, therefore, went on to testosterone replacement and puberty was therefore induced by drugs.

However, Harold would need to remain on testosterone replacement for the rest of his life and could not produce sperm.

The claimants argued that as Harold's testes had been high in the abdomen, there should have been a two-stage operation that would take cognisance of the potential problems of blood supply to testes if the blood vessels were under tension. If that had occurred, then although Harold would have undergone two operations, the testes would have been located in the scrotum with an adequate blood supply and would not have atrophied. He would then have been able to produce testosterone normally, go through puberty normally and also potentially father children. The defendants argued that the compromised blood supply was of no relevance as testicular atrophy had occurred for other reasons, such as mumps. At operation it was noted that the blood supply was adequate and the testes looked healthy.

The claimant's expert witness found that there was no evidence that Harold had ever had mumps and that infection of the testes leading to complete loss of testicular tissue without any symptoms was highly unlikely. Loss of testicular tissue following a one-stage operation on testes which were situated high in the abdomen was a recognised risk and, as such, the operation should have been undertaken in two stages. The defendants put forward no expert opinion and settled the case.

Female internal genitalia

The female internal genitalia consist of the uterus (womb), the fallopian tubes (tubes from the womb to the ovaries), and the ovaries themselves. During childhood, the internal genitalia are quiescent and it is not until puberty that there is enlargement of the uterus and activity within the ovaries. The oestrogen produced by the ovaries is important in breast development. Interaction between the two female hormones, oestrogen and progesterone, regulate the monthly periods. The maturation of an ovum, or egg, each month is accompanied by cyst formation on the ovary. These cysts can become greatly enlarged, causing abdominal discomfort. They can also twist, which causes acute abdominal pain, normally requiring surgical intervention and removal of the ovarian cyst.

Infection of the internal genitalia (pelvic inflammatory disease) is unusual in the paediatric age range. However, teenage sexual experimentation is increasing in numbers, with a large percentage of 16 year old boys and girls being sexually active. This may, therefore, lead to an increasing incidence of pelvic inflammatory disease as a cause of abdominal pain, as well as increasing the incidence of sexually transmitted diseases.

ABDOMINAL PAIN

Abdominal pain, or tummy ache, is a very common complaint in young children. Children under the age of seven or eight years have still not developed abstract thought, and so emotional distress may well be represented as physical pain, frequently tummy ache.

Abdominal pain can also be a manifestation of severe physical but also psychological pathology. The role, therefore, of GPs and paediatricians is to sift out those children who have abdominal pain that is as a result of severe pathology, in order that those children may be treated either physically or psychologically. This can indeed be most difficult. There are rough rules of thumb, but they are just that. There are no hard and fast guidelines for sorting out abdominal pain.

Any form of pain, be it abdominal or headache, that goes on for months or even years is unlikely to be caused by sinister or severe physical abnormality. Over that period of time, the pathology should have become manifest in other ways, such as weight loss, so the underlying cause would have been found.

Thus, abdominal pain associated with other symptoms, such as vomiting, anaemia, blood loss from the anus, or weight loss is more likely to be associated with pathology. The site of the pain can be useful. Pain situated around the umbilicus (belly button) tends not to be caused by physical pathology. The only organ around that area is the small intestine. All the other organs are placed at the 'edges' of the abdominal cavity. Thus, pain that is out towards the edges of the abdominal cavity, in the loins, for example, should be taken more seriously than vague central pain.

Abdominal pain is divided into two types, colicky and constant. Colicky pain is often described as squeezing pain, whereby the pain becomes really quite intense, but for a short period of time, and then wanes and in fact may disappear completely before coming back again, so it really is waves of acute pain. Constant abdominal pain is just that, there is no variation in the intensity of the pain. Colicky pain is associated with constipation or bloating, with a large amount of air or gas in the intestine, and may well be eased by either the passage of stool or wind.

Constant abdominal pain is more likely to be associated with infection or inflammation.

During the examination of the abdomen, care is taken not to hurt the child with abdominal pain, but it is important to try to elicit whether there is tenderness somewhere in the tummy. If there is an extreme reaction to having the abdomen pressed, then that gives the suggestion that there may be a psychological element. Tenderness in the flanks occurs in kidney infections. Tenderness in the bottom right corner of the abdomen occurs in appendicitis.

Examination is also important to determine whether there are any abnormal lumps in the abdomen. A 'lump' in the lower abdomen may be a pregnant uterus!

Examination of the anus and rectum is a normal part of a surgical examination of the abdomen, but it is not undertaken by paediatricians routinely. However, it is important to remember that in certain instances, abdominal pain itself, or abdominal pain secondary to constipation, may mask underlying sex abuse. Examination, therefore, of the anus and external genitalia is vital if a diagnosis of sex abuse is being considered.

Abdominal migraine

Abdominal migraine tends to occur in younger children, whereas migraine in the head occurs in older children (see Chapter 10). There is no particular age whereby abdominal migraine moves into migraine in the head, but children of six or seven tend to have abdominal migraine, if they suffer from migraine at all, and children of 9 or 10 tend to have cranial migraine.

There is commonly a family history of migraine, the child becomes deathly pale, as in cranial migraine, but then complains of abdominal pain rather than headache. Treatment is the same as for cranial migraine.

SURGICAL PROCEDURES

The end point of abdominal pain can be a surgical procedure, such as appendicectomy. Such procedures are outwith the remit of this book, but paediatricians are involved in the pre- and post-operative care of children, especially in district general hospitals where it is unusual to have dedicated paediatric surgeons. Most surgeons who operate on children are trained both in adult and paediatric surgery, but predominantly undertake surgery in adults, doing one or two lists a week only on children. Thus the perioperative care, especially fluid management, is best left to paediatricians.

The amount of fluid that children need varies considerably depending on their age and weight. A new-born baby requires 150 ml/kg/day of fluid. A large 14 year old will require only around 50 ml/kg/day. Thus, fluid management is more complicated than it is in adult practice, and great care must be taken when giving fluids, especially intravenous fluids, to babies and young children. Young children who are starved for a long time, either because they are waiting for operation or because the abdominal operation is such that they are unable to eat for several days, must also be given an adequate supply of sugar. They are less able to cope with starvation than adolescents and adults. So not only is the volume of fluid important but so also is the constitution of the fluid, which again is different from the fluids used routinely in adult practice. Care must therefore be taken to give the right type and the right amount of fluid to maintain normal levels of sodium, potassium and sugar in the bloodstream. Too little fluid and the child will become dehydrated and can go into kidney failure, too much fluid and the child may go into heart failure. Too little sugar and the child may have a fit.

Case study: failure to diagnose renal failure leading to wrong administration of fluids and eventual death

Shahid, aged 11, developed sudden, severe abdominal pain. The pain was colicky in nature in that it would rise to a crescendo before fading away, although it was always present. Shahid's father thought that it was indigestion, but after half an hour it was clear that Shahid was becoming quite unwell so his father took him to the Accident and Emergency department at the local hospital. It was clear that Shahid had severe pathology in his abdomen and was referred to the surgeons who, after making sure that Shahid was stable, operated upon him. At operation it was found that part of his gut had twisted and was dead. This part of the gut was removed and the two ends of the remaining gut sewn together.

After operation, it was noted that Shahid's blood pressure was very low and it was thought he had septicaemia (blood poisoning), because of the damage to his gut. He was treated with antibiotics and given intravenous fluids. He did not pass urine. It was thought that he was dehydrated, so the fluids going into his veins were increased in volume. Over the next few hours, he was still not passing urine and the fluids were increased further. He then required oxygen to keep his blood levels of oxygen correct, but found it difficult to breathe. Eventually he needed to be put on to a ventilator, but despite this it became impossible to maintain the right amount of oxygen and carbon dioxide in the blood and his blood pressure began to drop again. Despite intensive care, Shahid sadly died.

Shahid's father could not understand why a previously healthy lad, who only had a short period of abdominal pain, should die. He asked for an expert opinion independently.

Review of the intensive care notes revealed that the attending surgical staff failed to realise that Shahid had gone into kidney failure following a period of low blood pressure. They had mistakenly thought that Shahid's lack of urine output was related to dehydration. The fluids were therefore increased to a point where, for several hours, Shahid was receiving excessive fluids into his veins of 300 ml/kg/day.

This excess fluid had caused him to go into heart failure. His lungs had filled with fluid, requiring ventilation, and eventually causing his death.

Greater care should have been taken in making the diagnosis of kidney failure which, if correctly made, would have indicated decreased fluid requirements rather than increased. There was a high probability that the kidneys would have recovered by themselves, and that Shahid would have lived if there had not been excess fluid sending him into heart failure. The Trust did not contest the case.

CHAPTER 14

THE MUSCULO-SKELETAL SYSTEM

INTRODUCTION

The muscles and skeleton are considered together here, as they are clearly intimately related. The bones are articulated together and movement is effected by muscles being attached across joints. For example, the biceps muscle, which bends the elbow, is attached to the upper part of the humerus, the long bone between the shoulder and the elbow, and then to the radius, one of the bones in the forearm. Contraction, therefore, of the biceps pulls on the radius, so bending the elbow.

Facilitation of movement at the joint is via cartilage and synovial fluid. The cartilage adheres to the surface of the bones, as bones would not move well against each other, to provide a sort of rubber mount, and then the oil of the joint is the synovial fluid. The co-ordinated action of muscles and the smooth gliding of joints allows unencumbered and pain-free movement.

THE MUSCLE SYSTEM

The muscle fibres that make up the muscles have an ability to elongate and to contract. This ability allows muscles to change their length over joints, facilitating easy movement. For example, when the elbow is straight, the biceps muscle at the front of the arm is elongated and the triceps muscle, which is at the back of the arm and straightens the elbow, is shortened. As the elbow is bent, then the biceps muscle shortens and the triceps muscle elongates in a co-ordinated fashion. Muscles have two broad requirements in order to work: they need nerves to 'tell them' whether to contract or elongate, and the muscles themselves need to be healthy.

Nerve damage

If there is damage to the nerves of particular muscles, then the muscles cannot work in a co-ordinated fashion. Depending on where the damage to the nerves is, the muscles will either become lax (flaccid), or become tense (spastic).

The nervous system is divided into the central nervous system, which is the brain and the spinal cord, and the peripheral nervous system.

The spinal reflex

The peripheral nervous system consists of a loop of nerves. Nerves emanating from the spinal cord to the muscle transmit signals to the muscle to contract or elongate. The nervous system also needs to know the state of the muscle, so there is another nerve going from the muscle to the spinal cord relaying information about the muscle. This loop of nerves produces the spinal reflex. If there is no other influence on the nerves, the spinal nerve loop and reflex tries to stop the muscle moving. Thus there is resistance to any movement at the joint, be it active, that is, produced by the person themselves, or passive, when the joint is moved by somebody else. This is the basis for spasticity, which is seen in cases such as cerebral palsy. The spinal reflex is very powerful and tries to maintain the status quo. Any movement within muscles is resisted and the muscle goes into spasm, or is spastic.

Upper motor neurone damage

The role of the central nervous system, therefore, is to ameliorate the effects of the spinal reflex so that there is co-ordinated contraction and elongation of different muscles, allowing smooth movements at the joints. If there is damage, therefore, to the central nervous system, for example, in cerebral palsy, then the influence of the central nervous system on the spinal nerve loop and reflex is lost. The spinal reflex remains intact and those muscles affected become spastic. This is termed 'upper motor neurone damage'.

Lower motor neurone damage

The other type of damage, however, is when the peripheral nerves themselves are damaged and so there is no means for information from the spinal column or the brain to get to the muscles. In this case, the muscles lose their tone and become lax. This sort of damage is seen, for example, in damage to the brachial plexus in shoulder dystocia leading to Erb's palsy. The peripheral nerves are damaged and the arm hangs limply at the side of the child. It is possible, therefore, by examination and by determining the behaviour of muscles, to determine the site of damage to the nerves to the muscles, that is, whether it is central or whether it is peripheral, that is, upper or lower motor neurone damage.

Muscle effects of nerve damage

Muscles become developed only if they are used. In central damage leading to spasticity, then the muscles are always working and become more powerful. This is inco-ordinated because the muscles cannot be used voluntarily; it is merely the spinal reflex which causes the muscles to work constantly. This then leads to the characteristic deformities at joints.

Certain muscle groups are inherently more powerful than others. Those muscles that we need to resist gravity are more powerful than those that work with gravity. In the arms, for example, the biceps on the front of the arm, which pulls the forearm up against gravity, is more powerful than the triceps at the back of the arm, which works with gravity as the arm straightens. In the legs, it is the other way round, with the muscles in the front of the thighs, the quadriceps, which straighten the leg against gravity being more powerful than the muscles at the back of the leg, the hamstrings, which work with gravity. This explains the characteristic body position of children with a hemiplegia. The arm is flexed at the elbow and the leg is straightened out, with the toes pointing down so the child tends to walk on tiptoes.

There may also be abnormal deformities at joints with damaged peripheral nerves, in that those muscles with no nerve input have no power and cannot resist the inherent activity of those muscles with intact nerves. This leads to the characteristic position in children with Erb's palsy of a 'waiter's tip'. The muscles of the upper arm are affected, but not those of the lower arm. Thus the arm hangs down by the side but the forearm is twisted so that the fingers point backwards and are slightly flexed, as though awaiting a tip!

MUSCLE DAMAGE

Muscle damage can either be inherited or acquired.

Inherited muscle damage

Muscle fibres are complex, needing mechanisms to shorten and lengthen. They are made up of different chemicals in specific ratios in order for this to happen. If the muscles are inherently abnormal and weak, then the child is similarly weak. This may be obvious at birth, or it may become obvious as the child becomes older and the muscles become more and more affected. These are the so called 'myopathies', of which there are many and for which, at present, there is no cure.

Some are fatal within the first few months or years of life, such as Wernig Hoffman Syndrome, others in later childhood, such as Duchennes muscular dystrophy, which affects boys only. Others are compatible with a normal life span, although not normal muscle power. Diagnosis is made clinically and confirmed by a blood test or muscle biopsy.

No treatment is as yet possible. Once the diagnosis is made, care for these children is directed at relieving the effects of this inherited problem.

Acquired muscle damage

Acquired damage to muscles is usually traumatic. The muscle may be cut or crushed during an accident, or may be torn, such as during sport. Usually, unless the damage is extensive, repair can occur, although muscles heal by scar formation and the muscle will not be as strong as previously.

THE SKELETAL SYSTEM

The discussion on the skeletal system in this context of discussing the musculo-skeletal system will be confined to the joints between bones. Damage to and treatment of bony injuries is outwith the remit of this book. Damage to joints can either be acute or chronic.

Acute joint damage

Acute damage may be a result of trauma. A fracture to a bone may involve the joint itself, with the fracture running through the bone into the joint cavity, disrupting the surface of the bone within the joint. Treatment is directed at stabilising the fracture to reduce the damage to the joint surfaces. There is an increased incidence of later arthritis in adults in joints that have been so disrupted.

Joints, however, can be dislocated without damage to the bones on either side of the joint. This can occur relatively easily with fingers and with the shoulder. The shoulder has an enormous range of movement, but the price of having such flexibility is that the joint is relatively unstable, with the shoulder blade and the humerus being kept together by muscle power rather than the design of the joint. The opposite is true for the hip joint, which is extremely stable, with the head of the femur (long bone in the thigh) deep in a socket in the pelvis. Dislocation of a normal hip is therefore difficult, only occurring with major trauma such as in a road traffic accident. The hip always dislocates backwards, damaging the pelvis during dislocation. Again, people who have dislocated their joints as children may develop arthritis in adult life.

When dislocation occurs the muscles are stretched, which is not too much of a problem, but the ligaments that hold the joint together and the joint capsule, the envelope around the joint, also get stretched, so the joint becomes unstable. Treatment is therefore directed at stabilising the joint until the ligaments return to normal strength.

Septic arthritis

Joints have a relatively poor blood supply. The bone and cartilage overlying the bone require little in the way of nutrients or oxygen, and therefore joints require little in the way of blood supply. This has the advantage of reducing the chances of an infection within the joint, but has the disadvantage that once infection is there, then blood supply, and therefore antibiotic supply, to the joint to counteract the infection is poor.

Septic arthritis can, in theory, occur at any joint, although the joints most commonly affected are those in the limbs.

Diagnosis may be relatively easy. If one of the finger joints is infected, for example, it is easy to see. However, diagnosis may be quite difficult, for example, if the hip joint is infected, especially in young children. There is often nothing to see, although there may be resistance to the hip joint being moved. Rapid diagnosis is of considerable importance, as untreated septic arthritis can destroy the cartilage in the joint, disrupt the joint itself, and eventually infect the bone, leading to osteomyelitis. A young child with a temperature who resists movement at a particular joint should trigger in the mind of the paediatrician the possibility of a septic arthritis.

Case study: delayed diagnosis of osteomyelitis causing late asymmetry of the hands

Danny, aged four, was noticed by his parents to have swelling on the back of his right hand. The swelling was discoloured and they thought that he had bruised his hand or had been injured by one of his siblings. However, he was brought to the Accident and Emergency department and seen by the A & E consultant, who felt that there was a possibility of superficial infection (cellulitis) and treated him with an appropriate antibiotic, with the instruction to bring Danny back two days later, on Christmas Eve, for review.

At review, Danny's hand had become more swollen and he was referred to a consultant paediatrician. There was no history of trauma and no evidence of any entry wound, but the hand was very swollen and tender and Danny had a temperature. X-ray of the hand revealed nothing other than soft tissue swelling. The antibiotic dose was therefore increased and continued, with a follow-up appointment in the New Year.

Danny's hand had not improved in the intervening 10 days, despite taking antibiotics. It was, however, less painful and he was able to move his fingers more. Repeat x-ray revealed infection in four of the bones in Danny's hand (metacarpals), with possible infection of the joints.

He was admitted and treated with high-dose intravenous antibiotics and the infection was cleared. Follow-up revealed normal function and healing of the bones, but after two years Danny was left with different sized hands. The infection in Danny's right hand had increased the blood supply to the hand, which had grown more rapidly than his left hand. There was, however, normal strength and normal function.

The claimants argued that a diagnosis of osteomyelitis should have been made by the consultant paediatrician. Danny had had appropriate antibiotics for cellulitis which had not produced an improvement in two days, as would have been expected. It was therefore negligent to persist with a diagnosis of cellulitis and merely continue treatment for it. Had the appropriate diagnosis been made at the second consultation, then differential growth of the hands would not have occurred.

The defendants admitted liability but denied causation, arguing that osteomyelitis of four separate bones in the hand was already present at the second consultation and that the higher-dose antibiotic prescribed by the paediatrician would have had some effect at controlling infection. However, further discussion with the Trust's solicitor indicated that it was more cost-effective for the Trust to offer a modest settlement figure rather than to debate causation once liability had been admitted.

Chronic joint damage

Chronic arthritis

Children suffer from similar destructive arthritides of the joints as adults.

Reactive arthritis

Reactive arthritis occurs during or after a generalised infection, normally a viral infection. The child is generally but non-specifically unwell, and thereafter complains of joint pains and swelling. This usually occurs in the larger joints, such as the knees and the ankles, and tends to subside with the joint returning to normal shortly after the child improves from the generalised infection. However, this reactive arthritis may be recurrent, causing considerable pain and discomfort in those joints, but fortunately the joints do not become damaged. However, the child may be quite debilitated during the times of the attacks of arthritis.

A classical form of reactive arthritis is seen in rheumatic fever. The child suffers a bacterial infection with a particular organism, called *Streptococcus* Group A. This triggers the body's immune system, which may attack various organs in the body, including the joints. The joints affected are mainly the large joints, such as the knees and the ankles, and it is known as 'flitting arthritis'. Different joints may be affected on different days, with the joints apparently returning to normal whilst other joints become affected.

Juvenile chronic arthritis

Juvenile chronic arthritis (JCA) is quite similar to adult rheumatoid arthritis. It is an auto-immune disease whereby the body's own immune system attacks the joints, causing swelling, pain and destruction of the joints. Eventually there can be deformity of the joints and quite considerable limitation of movement, due to damage to the interior of the joint itself. There are different types of JCA: pauciarticular, when less than five joints are affected, and polyarticular, when five or more joints are affected. Different age groups and sexes have a propensity for different varieties of JCA, some including eye damage as well.

Less common arthritides

Arthritis may also be associated with generalised illnesses. It can occur as part of the skin disease, psoriasis, and this again can be a destructive arthritis.

Arthritis can also rarely be part of gut diseases, such as ulcerative colitis; the basis is again auto-immune.

Treatment for childhood arthritides

There are many different arthritidies and sub-divisions of the same type of arthritis, but fortunately relatively few children suffer from chronic arthritis. It is sensible, therefore, for shared care to be the model of care for these patients. The diagnosis needs to be confirmed at a tertiary centre and treatment modalities decided on. The drugs used can be effective but may have significant side effects, so alteration of medications and dosages is often best left to the specialist centre. Day to day care can, however, occur at the local secondary care unit.

Diagnosis may be quite difficult and it may also take some time for the diagnosis to be considered, especially in young children.

Case study: lost motor skills as a presentation of juvenile chronic arthritis

Gemma was the first child of Anthony and Judith. The pregnancy had been entirely normal and Gemma's development had been carefully monitored by her parents as well as by the Child Health Surveillance Scheme. She started walking at 13 months of age, and by 15 months had discovered how to climb out of her cot. She would do this in the early hours of the morning and race around to her parents' bedroom.

Gemma's parents noticed one day that they had slept through the entire night. Gemma had ceased climbing out of her cot, much to the relief of her parents, who slept well. However, they then began to notice that Gemma was very slow in walking in the mornings, but by mid morning she was up to her normal speed. Gemma was taken along to her GP and they were reassured that this was just normal toddler behaviour. However, Gemma's parents became increasingly concerned that she was not really developing her gross motor skills; although she was walking, she was not running and was really quite slow in the morning. She would complain bitterly if her mother tried to hurry her up. Her parents asked for a referral to the local paediatrician. Examination revealed swelling of two joints in Gemma's hand, but also swelling of her left knee and right ankle. A possible diagnosis of juvenile chronic arthritis was made by the paediatrician and Gemma was referred immediately to the tertiary centre. Fortunately, she responded well to treatment.

Gemma's parents claimed that the GP who had missed the diagnosis should have referred Gemma earlier to the paediatrician. This would have led to earlier diagnosis and prevented several weeks of pain and discomfort. However, in discussion with the expert witness and Counsel, it was agreed that there would have been no difference in response to treatment had Gemma been referred those few weeks earlier. She suffered no joint damage and therefore there was no case for causation. The chances of success with regard to the case for Gemma's discomfort was not considered sufficiently robust to warrant continued legal aid.

CHAPTER 15

SUDDEN UNEXPECTED DEATH SYNDROME (SUDS)

INTRODUCTION

Sudden unexpected death can occur at any age. Indeed, a sudden unexpected death from heart attack is one of the commonest forms of death in middle-aged men. However, the U in SUDS should stand not only for unexpected, but also for unexplained. Thus, infants, children and adults who suffer from SUDS have no cause for their sudden demise found at post mortem. SUDS can therefore be used as a sort of generic term, and has in some areas taken over from age-related acronyms such as SIDS (sudden infant death syndrome) and SADS (sudden adult or adolescent death syndrome).

DEFINITION OF SUDS

The definition of SUDS, therefore, is sudden unexpected death in a previously healthy child in whom no explanation can be found, either clinically or at post mortem. SUDS can also occur in children who have previously been unwell, for example, they may have a heart problem, but the particular heart problem was not the cause of the sudden demise.

CAUSE OF SUDS

There is much debate as to the cause of SUDS in infancy, which is still the commonest cause of sudden death in children under the age of one year. The peak age for SUDS is less than six months, but it can occur up to, and in fact slightly beyond, one year of life.

A typical history is that an infant has been previously well, fed normally, changed, tucked up in bed and then found dead a few hours later. There is not usually a sign of struggle, the bedclothes are normally undisplaced and so the infant just died quietly and peacefully. There have been reports of SUDS in infants in carrycots in the back of cars, and also in infants in baby units in hospitals. Thus the presence of adults is no guarantee against a child suffering from SUDS.

There has been much debate as to the cause of SUDS. It is felt to be multifactorial, with the various factors leading to a common end, which is circulatory collapse and cessation of heartbeat. Many environmental factors have been considered. However, the one change that has produced the most dramatic fall in incidence is the 'Back to sleep' campaign, where infants are placed on their backs to sleep.

'Back to sleep'

This is an interesting reinvention of the wheel, in that a generation ago infants were placed on their backs to sleep. This was felt then to be dangerous because if infants vomited they could inhale their own vomitus, and infants were then placed on their fronts to sleep. That move seems to have cost many lives. This simple alteration appears to have reduced the incidence of sudden infant death syndrome from one in 500 infants to about one in 1,000 infants.

THE CARE OF THE NEXT INFANT (CONI)

Suffering the devastation of SUDS in the family unfortunately increases the chances of a subsequent child also suffering from SUDS. The chances are at least doubled, if not more, of the subsequent sibling suffering SUDS. This increase has led to the formation of CONI. This is a national programme normally overseen by community health workers, often health visitors, where there is considerable care taken of the subsequent sibling.

The sorts of measures that may be involved are frequent visiting of the family, frequent weighing of the infant (there does appear to be an association between weight loss and SUDS) and also the possibility of using apnoea alarms. These are alarms attached to the baby, which detect breathing movements and click each time the baby takes a breath. If there is cessation of breathing the apnoea alarm sounds, alerting the adult carers. There is, however, considerable controversy as to whether the use of apnoea alarms does actually reduce the incidence of SUDS.

EXPLICABLE SUDS

Post mortem investigation in infants suffering from SUDS have tended to concentrate on looking for areas of obvious infection, such as pneumonia or gastroenteritis, but sometimes have not looked for the more subtle causes and, indeed, have sometimes missed some rather blatant causes. Such causes may include non-accidental injury that leads on to infanticide; there may have been hitherto unrecognised potentially lethal defects, especially in the heart; or there may be lethal errors of metabolism. The last relates to the way that infants digest and utilise foodstuffs. If this is inadequate, or if certain foodstuffs cannot be utilised effectively because of a deficiency of enzymes, then toxic waste can accumulate in the body, causing death.

Placing infants on their back has reduced the incidence of SUDS, but not to zero. In an attempt to gain greater understanding of possible causes of SUDS, some areas have embarked on investigative projects in the hope of gaining elucidation. In Birmingham, the Coroner established a protocol whereby all infants following SUDS had standardised investigations looking for previously unknown metabolic causes, and had a post mortem undertaken by highly specialised paediatric pathologists. As yet no data is available as to the frequency of explicable sudden death that was not detected ante mortem.

Congenital abnormalities

Antenatal screening

Virtually all mothers undergo ultrasound scans during pregnancy. The purpose of these scans is to determine the approximate size and growth rate of the fetus, but more importantly to try to detect significant congenital abnormalities before birth. Ultrasonography is undertaken in all district general hospitals. These should include detailed scans looking specifically for abnormalities in the heart, brain and kidneys, as well as of the limbs. If such abnormalities are suspected, then referral should be made to a specialist centre. For example, paediatric cardiologists are now undertaking ultrasounds of the heart of the fetus. This is an attempt to elucidate congenital abnormalities before birth so that the families can be prepared and also, if necessary, medical intervention planned early.

Postnatal screening

All children born in hospital have a thorough examination in the first 24–48 hours of life. The examination includes checking for all external features, including the stability of the hips, but also listening to the heart and palpating the abdomen. This again is a screening check to try to determine whether an infant does have any congenital abnormalities.

There are significant changes in circulation between the fetus and the new-born baby. It takes time for these various changes to settle down completely and so abnormalities in the heart may not be heard in the first 24–48 hours. Infants, therefore, attend a health surveillance check at six weeks of age at which, amongst other things, the heart is listened to again. There is, therefore, considerable effort to detect abnormalities in infants. Unfortunately, despite all these checks, abnormalities can still slip through the net.

Case study: severe cardiac abnormality mimicking sudden unexpected death syndrome in infancy

Nabila was the first-born daughter of a 20 year old Indian woman and her 33 year old husband. The pregnancy had been planned and the birth greeted with joy. The pregnancy had been uneventful; the ultrasound scans had been in concordance with menstrual dates. Immediate examination after birth revealed a normal, healthy daughter. At five weeks of age, Nabila's mother took her to the GP as Nabila was beginning to vomit. The GP examined Nabila's abdomen and felt that it was rather distended. He felt she had swallowed air and recommended that Nabila should be given Infacol and Fennel water.

The following morning, Nabila's father was concerned about the worsening distension of her abdomen. Nabila was undressed whilst being fed by her mother as her parents were unsure as to why her abdomen was so distended. Nabila suddenly stopped breathing and her parents could not induce her to breathe again. They dialled 999 and Nabila arrived at the Accident and Emergency department some 20 minutes later. By this time, she was cold at 33°C (normal 37°C), she was not breathing and had a heart rate of 40 beats per minute detected on the monitor, but no blood pressure. She was immediately intubated and cardiac massage begun. However, after 30 minutes of intensive resuscitation, a blood pressure could not be achieved and Nabila's heart rate remained at around 60 beats per minute. A decision was made to stop resuscitation.

At post mortem, a gross abnormality of the heart was detected. On closer questioning, it became clear that Nabila's mother had been concerned almost from birth at the rapidity of Nabila's breathing. Nabila had slipped into heart failure within the first few days of life, secondary to her cardiac abnormality. Her liver had enlarged greatly secondary to her heart failure, causing the distension of her abdomen. Eventually the heart failed to pump blood effectively at the point when Nabila's mother was feeding her, causing loss of circulation, loss of oxygen to the brain, and sudden collapse.

The claimants argued that the cardiac abnormality should have been detected on ultrasound scan or, failing that, should have been detected at the first baby check. Expert advice was sought and it was clear that antenatal ultrasonography did not detect 100% of cardiac abnormalities, nor did the first baby check. Indeed, the recognition of the latter point was embodied in the need for the six-week check. On discussion with counsel, the case did not continue.

NON-ACCIDENTAL INJURY/INFANTICIDE

Non-accidental injury is a sad but recurring theme within our society. On occasion, the assault on the child can lead to death. The parents can be so frustrated by a crying infant that they may shake the child in a fit of uncontrollable anger. The parents themselves may be very tired after sleepless nights and the constant crying may be more than can be borne. The child is grabbed around the chest and shaken violently backwards and forwards. The baby is unable to control its head well, and the head rocks violently backwards and forwards. This causes sheering of the blood vessels between the skull and the brain, leading to internal haemorrhage. This can be sufficiently severe to cause death. An associated feature of the 'shaken baby syndrome' is retinal haemorrhage. These are bleeds into the retina at the back of the eye, which can be seen using an ophthalmoscope. However, the child itself may have no signs of injury. If the child is clothed, there may be no bruising on the chest and there may be no abnormalities visible to the head, so to the unwary this may be another case of SUDS.

The true incidence of infant murder by adults is unknown. There are some authors who feel it is quite common. There are others who are more circumspect. However, it is a recognised cause of sudden death and is a diagnosis that is considered in the Birmingham experiment, when all post mortems are undertaken centrally.

Babies may be brought in dead, which is the first time they have been in contact with the medical profession since birth, but frequently there have been warning visits. A child may have been admitted previously with an unexplained 'funny turn' (acute life threatening event). No cause might be found in hospital, and the child discharged and then be brought in moribund or dead subsequently.

Acute life threatening event (ALTE)

Unexplained concerning events should be investigated appropriately. The child may come in with a history of a fit, a history of going apnoeic (stopping breathing), or choking. A careful history should be taken, which should include whether these events have occurred previously, and a decision made as to whether the child should be admitted for observation and investigation. Unfortunately now, admitting paediatricians should be very suspicious of non-accidental injury in all infants and children who have unexplained 'funny turns'. It is better to err on the side of caution and to acquire social work advice unnecessarily in innocent cases, rather than miss potentially life threatening adult-perpetrated events. Observation in hospital of the parent/child interaction may be helpful. Covert surveillance may be revealing.

Covert surveillance

The use of covert surveillance in hospital is enveloped in controversy. On the one hand, there are those who feel that secret videoing of parents is a gross invasion of their privacy. On the other, there are those who believe that any invasion of parental privacy is worth the life of a child. There is, as yet, no universally accepted national guidance as to the acceptability of covert surveillance.

There have, however, been dramatic videos of parents partially smothering their children in hospital. The smothering continues until the child fits from lack of oxygen to the brain, whereupon the pillow is removed. This covert surveillance has been used more to uncover the problem of Munchausen's Syndrome by Proxy, but could conceivably be used in uncovering the cause of acute life threatening events. Munchausen's Syndrome by Proxy is the falsification of illness by parents in their children. This frequently leads to unnecessary and sometimes extensive investigation of children into a fictitious disease.

SUDS in infancy has multiple and possibly interlinked causes. Further research is needed to try to pare away those infants for whom a cause can be found, leaving a nucleus of children who truly have a sudden unexpected and unexplained death for whom even further research is necessary.

SUDS AND EPILEPSY

There is an increased incidence of SUDS in epilepsy. It is an association which has been determined by analysing the death rate in children and adults with epilepsy and those without epilepsy. SUDS is entirely unpredictable; it is unclear whether it is the end point of an epileptic fit, although many feel it is not. SUDS can also happen whether the child is on or off treatment. Fortunately, although the incidence of SUDS is increased in children in epilepsy, it is still extremely rare (see case study, p 89).

CHAPTER 16

PAEDIATRIC INTENSIVE CARE

INTRODUCTION

The natural expectation of all parents is that their children will outlive them; that is the natural progression of life. However, that sadly does not always occur and some children do become very ill and require intensive care. The absolute need of paediatric intensive care, however, is far less in terms of numbers than adult intensive care. The majority of children are looked after in general hospitals, either in district general hospitals or in tertiary centres, but as part of a general hospital caring for both children and adults. There are relatively few isolated paediatric hospitals left in the UK, and there is much debate as to whether such isolated units should exist.

INTENSIVE CARE UNITS

The main criterion for admission to intensive care is the need for ventilatory support, normally undertaken by anaesthetists. Before this critical stage, most adults and children are cared for by physicians or surgeons on the general wards. The need for intensive care involves a move to the intensive care unit. Thus, anaesthetists have traditionally played either a major role, or indeed taken over care completely, of patients entering both adult and paediatric intensive care units.

Neonatal intensive care units

There is a reluctance to readmit babies to neonatal intensive care units once they have been discharged, because they have picked up various bacteria and viruses from the community and are therefore considered 'dirty' as compared with babies admitted to the neonatal unit directly from the maternity unit. This concern is greatly heightened if a baby is admitted with an infectious disease, so such babies tend to be admitted to a paediatric ICU. Hence the age range, and more importantly the size range, of children admitted for intensive care varies considerably from a 4 or 5 kg six week old through to an 80 kg 14 year old! The medical care and medical requirements vary enormously between these two extremes, far more than is generally experienced in the adult population. It could be argued, therefore, that paediatric intensivists need a broader band of experience than adult intensivists.

Paediatric and adult intensive care units

Case mix

The specialist paediatric hospitals with paediatric intensive care units used to look after children from the major specialties, such as oncology and cardiology. Often the expectation of survival was not high. In contradistinction, those children entering adult intensive care units in district general hospitals were previously well and had suffered an acute insult. The expectation of survival was therefore very high.

Comparative death rates

The type of care needed for a six week old baby is completely different from that of an 80 kg 14 year old, who is effectively an adult and can be managed totally appropriately in an adult intensive care unit. Small babies need minute attention to detail with respect to temperature control and fluid control, and also are managed by a type of ventilation, pressure limited, as opposed to the volume limited type of ventilation used in adults. The difference between these two types of ventilation is broadly that pressure controlled ventilation means that air and oxygen is blown into the baby's lungs until a particular pressure is reached; the pressure cannot be exceeded. This means, for example, that babies with soft pliant lungs will have a large volume of air delivered to them, whereas babies who have very stiff lungs, for example, in generalised chest infections, would only have a relatively small volume of air delivered to their lungs, as the lungs are unable to expand much and therefore the pressure is reached rapidly. In volume dependent ventilation, a pre-set volume is delivered to the patient regardless of the pressure generated within the lungs. This has the advantage of making sure that adequate air and oxygen is delivered to the lungs, but it has the disadvantage of allowing potentially very high pressure within the lungs that can itself cause damage.

This difference of approach across the paediatric age range is potentially not well managed in a unit used to adult intensive care. In a district general hospital there may be several hundred adults cared for during a year, whereas there may only be 20–40 children per year, and of those, there may be very few who are younger than one year of age.

Comparative survival data between tertiary dedicated paediatric intensive care units and children nursed on adult intensive care units in Australia revealed that there was an unexpectedly high death rate in the district general hospitals. This data did compare like with like and came to the conclusion that paediatric intensive care units gave a better service to children than adult intensive care units. The reasons for this are complex and difficult to unravel, but one area that does cause considerable concern is fluid balance in small infants and children (see case study, p 65).

This data caused much controversy and there was considerable debate as to whether data generated in a country such as Australia, with relatively few large units for children and many geographically scattered smaller units, was applicable to the UK. However, some areas in the UK developed a policy that no children should be cared for in an adult intensive care unit and that all children must be referred into a paediatric intensive care unit. This, however, creates other difficulties, in that there can be no guarantee that a paediatric intensive care bed can always be found. There are also concerns about district general paediatric units losing the requisite skills to resuscitate and stabilise critically sick children before transport to the tertiary centre. There are also difficulties in safely transporting critically ill children between hospitals in the unstable environment of an ambulance.

Case study: rigid intensive care policy leading to avoidable death

Following the data from the Australian paediatric intensive care units, a region in the UK decreed that all children requiring intensive care must be transferred to the paediatric intensive care unit and that children must no longer be admitted to the adult intensive care units.

A paediatric intensive care unit existed in the tertiary centre, but there was no provision for increased paediatric beds and there was no provision for safe transfer of children needing intensive care.

Rebecca, a nine year old child, was admitted to a district general hospital suffering from meningococcal septicaemia (blood poisoning caused by the meningitis bacterium). She had been well the previous night but on awakening had felt shivery, was complaining of a headache, and her mother then noticed a couple of spots on her chest. She was, however, relatively well. Her mother took her immediately to the local district general hospital Accident and Emergency department, where the diagnosis of meningococcal septicaemia was promptly made and Rebecca was given a first dose of appropriate intravenous antibiotics. Examination revealed that there were now several spots over her chest, that she was becoming drowsier, but that her blood pressure was maintained.

Over the next three hours, however, Rebecca's condition deteriorated and the rash spread rapidly, despite antibiotics. She herself became confused and her blood pressure began to drop. She was treated with increased fluids to maintain her blood pressure, but this did not succeed and she was then started on intravenous drugs to maintain her blood pressure. Despite this, her blood pressure continued to drift downwards. It was felt that she needed to be transferred to an intensive care unit and the paediatric intensive care unit was contacted. No beds were available in the regional centre, nor were any paediatric beds available in the next paediatric intensive care centre some 60 miles away.

Admission to the adult intensive care unit was requested, but adherence to the protocol dictated that the child be refused admission.

There were no facilities on the general paediatric ward to give Rebecca ventilatory support, even in the short term. It was felt, therefore, that she could not be intubated because if this occurred, the only ventilatory approach would be by manual ventilation by an anaesthetist, which could not continue for hours as there was no obvious paediatric bed available.

Rebecca's inexorable decline continued and sadly she died.

At inquest it was felt that this was an avoidable death, and both the regional centre and the district general hospital were subject to a professional review by the Royal College of Physicians. The professional review was highly critical of a rigid protocol that had effectively deskilled the district general hospital, which was no longer able to look after sick children even for a short time without guaranteed provision of intensive care at the centre.

Following that report, Rebecca's parents put in a claim against the district general hospital for Rebecca's death, which was not contested.

THE DOBSON REPORT

High-profile paediatric deaths or frantic ambulance journeys across England in an attempt, often unsuccessfully, to find paediatric intensive care beds, prompted the Labour Government to produce a solution. Frank Dobson was Secretary of State for Health at that time, and commissioned a report on how to safely provide paediatric intensive care. The paediatric group included paediatric anaesthetists, intensive care paediatricians and also general paediatricians.

Paediatric intensive care

The broad recommendations were that there should be three levels of intensive care available to all children, but not in all hospitals.

Level 1

Level 1 care must be available in all hospitals. All hospitals must be able to stabilise very sick children and maintain vital signs until a child is safely transferred to the paediatric intensive care unit.

Level 2

In large district general hospitals which have an active adult intensive care unit, but also sufficiently large numbers of children (greater than 40 per year) looked after in such units, should continue to support the tertiary paediatric intensive care units by looking after children on adult intensive care units.

Level 3

Level 3 paediatric intensive care units (PICUs) are able to look after any manner of problem in all ages of children and infants, other than neonates, who should be looked after on a neonatal intensive care unit. They should be staffed by dedicated paediatric anaesthetists and intensive care trained paediatricians.

There must be clear protocols and agreement between hospitals providing Level 2 care, which is effectively for previously healthy children, and Level 3 paediatric intensive care units, so that if children in the Level 2 units deteriorate, there are clear guidelines for transfer to the more experienced paediatric intensive care centres (see case study, p 65).

Although not mandatory, many large paediatric intensive care units now have dedicated PICU ambulances and retrieval squads that consist of doctors and nurses. These retrieval squads will go out to the district general hospitals and will help the local staff stabilise the child before transfer back to the centre. However, it may be several hours before a retrieval team can get to a district general hospital. This may be because they are busy at another hospital or because the local PICU is full and the child needs to be transferred further afield. Hence the great importance of not deskilling district general hospitals with regard to looking after sick children, and the necessity for district general hospitals to be able to look after and stabilise sick children for a matter of hours. This can be a difficult balance to achieve, but should be one that is accomplished by collaboration between the local hospital and the tertiary PICU centre.

INDEX

G

H

I

J

K

L